Penguin Masterstudies
Advisory Editors:
Stephen Coote and Bryan Loug

F. Scott Fitzgerald

Tender is the Night

Kathleen Parkinson

Penguin Books

Penguin Books Ltd, Harmondsworth, Middlesex, England
Viking Penguin Inc., 40 West 23rd Street, New York, New York 10010, U.S.A.
Penguin Books Australia Ltd, Ringwood, Victoria, Australia
Penguin Books Canada Ltd, 2801 John Street, Markham, Ontario, Canada L3R 1B4
Penguin Books (N.Z.) Ltd, 182–190 Wairau Road, Auckland 10, New Zealand

First published 1986

Made and printed in Great Britain by
Richard Clay (The Chaucer Press) Ltd, Bungay, Suffolk
Filmset in 9/11pt Monophoto Times by
Northumberland Press Ltd, Gateshead, Tyne and Wear

Contents

Acknowledgements   7

1. *Tender is the Night*: A Novel of the 1920s   9
   Fitzgerald's career as a novelist   9
   The writing of *Tender is the Night*, 1925–34   11
   The reception of the novel   14
   The Malcolm Cowley edition   15
   The First World War and its aftermath in
       contemporary writing   16
   The post-war world as wasteland   20
   The prosperous 1920s: a wasteland of wealth   21
   International travel   25
   The Jazz Age: universal entertainment for restless people   27
   Developments in modern psychology   30

2. The Time-scheme of the Novel   34
   A summary of events in the order of narration   34
   The period of time covered by the novel   39
   Book I as the crux of the time-scheme   40

3. Dick Diver   47
   'The Crack-Up'   47
   Young Dr Richard Diver   48
   The mature Dick Diver   52
   Significant points relating to Dick Diver   53

4. Women Characters: 'You Are Attractive to Women, Dick'   61
   The unnamed woman patient   61
   American women   62
   Baby Warren   62
   Mrs Elsie Speers   64
   Mary North   66
   Rosemary Hoyt   69
   He 'was much admired by the ladies'   75
   Nicole Diver   75

5. The Structure of *Tender is the Night*   81

The function of violence, death and aggression in the novel   83

The contribution of settings to mood in the first half of the novel   87

The title of the novel   90

The process of dehumanization in the second half of the novel   91

Switzerland and the Riviera   94

Nicole's garden   96

Changing points of view: an important structural feature   97

Notes   102

Selected Reading   104

Acknowledgements

The edition used in this study of *Tender is the Night* is the Penguin edition of 1982, edited by Arnold Goldman, to whom grateful acknowledgement for use is made.

All quotations are taken from this edition.

1. *Tender is the Night*: A Novel of the 1920s

Set among an exclusive group of expatriate Americans enjoying all the privileges and luxuries of their wealth in Europe during the 1920s, *Tender is the Night* not only reflects many of the features of the period, it also makes them an integral part of its narrative processes. A novel of the 1920s, it is of the 1920s too in its experimental handling of psychoanalytic insights, characterized by the use of a complicated time structure and by the creation of vivid images of the post-war period as a means of reflecting inner worlds of mood and feeling. In a letter written in 1932, Fitzgerald cited Jung, a founding figure of the modern study of the unconscious mind, as the contemporary who best understood the twentieth-century world 'into which willy-nilly one's children will grow up'. For Fitzgerald recognized the alienation of the individual from contemporary society: 'I think we are all a little sick but the logic of history won't permit us to go backwards.'[1] The novel represents his artistic attempt to find a contemporary style which could express the modern consciousness.

Since Fitzgerald's own life also reflects the decade, an account of the nine years during which the novel took shape will form an introduction to this study.

Fitzgerald's career as a novelist

Success came early to Scott Fitzgerald, with the publication of his first novel, *This Side of Paradise*, in 1920. For a young man of twenty-four, recently demobbed from the army, who was dependent on his writing for a living and who had, not so long before, had to put cardboard in his shoes, publication meant the satisfaction of knowing that he could write. A further happy result of this was that Zelda Sayre, whom he met while he was an officer in the army, and who had so far refused him, agreed to marry him now that his future seemed assured. Even so, for a young couple given to extravagant living, the sales of novels did not bring in enough money, and Fitzgerald quickly found that he could command higher prices and fast cash for his short stories. A recent biographer expresses the dilemma which, as a serious novelist, Fitzgerald faced all through the 1920s.

As a writer, Fitzgerald had to live by the pendulum because as soon as he stopped grinding out pulp for the big magazines and turned to serious writing, he found himself on the brink of financial disaster. His independence was measured by the number of stories he had to produce each year. But his dependence increased with his needs, which grew grander by the year; the temptation to take the easy way was reinforced by the rapidly rising fees he commanded, especially from the [*Saturday Evening*] *Post*.[2]

It is significant that a good story like 'The Diamond as Big as the Ritz' (see the Penguin collection of stories published under that name) was refused by this magazine because it was critical of American materialism. Only optimistic stories were wanted for popular consumption.

Fitzgerald was regarded by readers of the *Post* as the writer who best represented the young post-war generation of ambitious middle-class Americans wanting to enjoy the new consumer spending boom of the 1920s. His stories seemed to express the dream world which advertising was busy building, the world of jazz and dancing, of young heroines who were essentially modern and who bobbed their hair, smoked and drank, of romantic night life; above all, his characters were consumers who spent lavishly and extravagantly. As its most successful contributor of stories, Fitzgerald helped to create the rapid success of this magazine.

In their early married life, the Fitzgeralds came to embody the new Jazz Age, and Fitzgerald wrote both himself and his wife into his short stories and into his next novel, *The Beautiful and Damned* (1922). But both drank heavily and they were often in debt, despite the money Fitzgerald made from the film rights of several of his stories. There seems to have been a mutually destructive drive in their relationship, as each egged the other on to extremes of rashness and irresponsibility, yet each needed the other, too. It was around this time that Fitzgerald began to feel increasingly concerned about the waste of his talents. As a writer who was sensitive to the age, and who was regarded as its spokesman, he wanted to be a serious critic of his society. Already in 1922, when he was twenty-five years old, he was writing in his diary: 'A bad year. No work. Slow deteriorating depression with outbreak around the corner.'[3]

The early 1920s in the United States were the period of rapid consumer-goods expansion. They also saw the introduction in 1920 of Prohibition, which was an attempt to limit the manufacture and sale of alcohol. Its effect, particularly during this period of increased wealth, new film and radio entertainment, and increased mobility through the massive development of the automobile industry, was to create a wave of crime on an unprecedented scale. Bootlegging – the manufacture and sale of illicit liquor – created gang warfare, corrupted some of the police and instituted a major outbreak of organized crime. Fitzgerald's third novel,

The Great Gatsby (1925), reflects that world, but it puts it into the wider context of the American Dream. The vision of a New World that had inspired the settlers in America and that had once been bright and beautiful in its promise of fulfilment, had gone awry and turned into a nightmare world of violence.

The Great Gatsby was well received by the critics, but its sales were not high. The rights from stage and screen adaptations, however, brought in considerable financial rewards in 1926. By this time the Fitzgeralds had travelled abroad and begun to live in Italy and France. Fitzgerald had already begun work on what was eventually to become *Tender is the Night*, and in late 1926 he wrote to his agent:

> The book is wonderful – I honestly think that when it's published I shall be the best American novelist (which isn't saying a lot) but the end seems far away ... You remember I used to say I wanted to die at thirty – well, I'm now twenty-nine and the prospect is still welcome. My work is the only thing that makes me happy – except to be a little tight – and for those two indulgences I pay a big price in mental and physical hangovers.[4]

The desire to be 'the best American novelist' is a measure of his ambition. Certainly *Tender is the Night* is extremely ambitious in scale: it reflects a particular period of time, the post-First World War years, and in presenting an enormous spread of people, all Americans, attempts to portray the dilemmas of American identity in the modern world. Even though the novel is set in Europe, it encompasses a great deal of American life and American values. Yet Fitzgerald was increasingly modest about the value of his work, particularly when he measured himself against the ascending star of his younger American contemporary, Ernest Hemingway, whom he both helped initially and admired. As for references to dying at thirty, in fact he lived to be forty-four, the last dozen or so years being spent in Hollywood working on scripts. He left an unfinished novel, *The Last Tycoon*, which is set in Hollywood during the highly politicized 1930s, and which, as always, contains many autobiographical elements. By that time Fitzgerald regarded himself as a forgotten novelist: when, shortly before his death, he tried to buy a set of his works for a friend, he discovered they were not even on sale any more.

The writing of *Tender is the Night*, 1925–34

Fitzgerald began working on the novel in the summer of 1925, the time at which the narrative also begins, with Rosemary's arrival with her mother at Gausse's Hotel on the French Riviera just outside Cannes. This was the period in which Fitzgerald and his wife Zelda were themselves experiencing the world of expatriate American life in Paris and on the Riviera, in company with other American writers, artists and film-stars. The exchange rate of the dollar was extremely favourable to Americans in the 1920s, and Europe, particularly Paris, was a magnet for artists in all fields of activity. The Fitzgeralds were still enjoying the esteem which his novels and short stories had brought, as well as the financial security, but the tensions and private insecurities in their lives were exacerbated when the money began to give out. They engaged in an extravagant life-style during their years in Paris and on the Riviera, which included travel to Rome and North Africa. In 1924 in Rome they met the American cast of a spectacular MGM version of the novel *Ben-Hur*, which is set in ancient Rome, and became friendly with the stars. Zelda noticed that the plaster arenas were bigger than the real ones, just as Dick Diver does when he visits the set of Rosemary's film, *The Grandeur that was Rome* (Book II, p. 231). Fitzgerald, again like Dick, was involved in a night-club brawl and a fight with taxi-drivers, and on another occasion was thrown into prison and beaten up by the Roman police. Back on the Riviera, he was frequently drunk and played rather juvenile tricks on people, at one point even wanting to saw a waiter in half, as Abe North does in the novel (Book I, p. 41). As always in his fiction, it would be easy to name any number of incidents that were autobiographical in origin, including Zelda's affair with a young French officer and his own friendship with a young American film-star travelling with her mother. But the exercise would be pointless, since what matters is the significance of these incidents within the artistic structure and their place in the pattern of events in the narrative.

For example, the opening of the novel on the beach of Gausse's Hotel in 1925 catches a particular moment in social history as well as a particular period in Fitzgerald's own life, but its significance in the novel is that it marks an important point in the life of the central character, Dick Diver. Historically, this was the period when wealthy Americans were transforming the Riviera into a fashionable international summer resort. Fictionally, it is the point when Dick is to be tempted by the youth of Rosemary and her admiration for himself, the point when the image he has built of himself is beginning to crack.

The Fitzgeralds were themselves guests on the Riviera in 1925 of two wealthy Americans, Gerald and Sara Murphy, whose house at Antibes just outside Cannes, the Villa America, became the model for the Divers' Villa Diana. The Murphys were great party-givers who set the social pattern for fashionable living on the Riviera during the summer months and contributed to the transformation of the beach into the haunt of the very rich. Gerald Murphy even raked a portion of the beach, just as Dick does (Book I, p. 15). They were on friendly terms with many of the internationally famous artists of the period, Picasso for one, and gave the Fitzgeralds access to some of the world's most notable people. Fitzgerald, however, did not merely catch this phenomenon of the new social pleasures of a leisured class who were discovering the delights of sun and beach, he made it of structural importance in the opening and closing scenes of the novel. The beach which Rosemary's gaze takes in in 1925 at the opening of the novel has suffered an invasion by 1929 when the novel ends. By 1929 it is seen to be vulgarized, taken over by the publicity-seekers and the society photographers (Book III, p. 334) who follow in the wake of the élite. The old intimacy which characterized the Divers and their set at the beginning of the novel has vanished. The Divers 'invented this beach' (Book I, p. 26) and enjoyed its pleasures by means of an enviable exclusiveness, but the sense of style they gave it has been lost by 1929. Fitzgerald thus drew on his own experiences of the contemporary social scene to make the last four years of the decade – the summer of 1925 to the summer of 1929 – the material of Dick Diver's personal tragedy.

Although Fitzgerald began working on the novel in 1925, it was not completed for publication until 1934, and during those nine years of its composition it underwent a number of major changes. He planned first of all a story about a young American technician in the film industry who was to murder his mother while living and working on the Riviera. A second plot involving a fashionable couple and a young film-star was superimposed on this, and it was only in a draft version of 1932 that the Divers emerged as the central figures in the narrative. Thus by 1932 Fitzgerald was in a position to achieve a comprehensive view, one both personal and historical, of the whole previous decade. Unfortunately this was largely as a result of the emotional problems, as well as the problems of composition, he suffered during the nine years in which the novel took shape. As far as his personal life was concerned, Fitzgerald would thus have probably viewed this period as anything but fruitful, since it was a time of struggle for both himself and Zelda. The tensions between them grew worse: he was forced to continue writing for magazines for ready cash and he feared constantly that he could not sustain his literary talent. In 1930 Zelda, who had already attempted suicide, suffered her first mental breakdown and required expensive treatment in a sanatorium in Montreux; this was followed by a second breakdown and further treatment in the United States in 1932. One of her symptoms was a rash of eczema over her whole body, which had to be swathed in bandages, and must have provided Fitzgerald with a poignant model for the mental patient whose plight moves Dick Diver so unbearably in Book II (p. 202). The drain on Fitzgerald's own mental and emotional energies was considerable.

Undoubtedly Fitzgerald wrote much of himself and Zelda into this novel. His notes record that he drew upon Zelda's case for some of the medical treatment for Nicole's illness. His own fear of failure, both as a writer and in his emotional life, and his anxiety over Zelda's mental instability, must have helped him to create the poignancy of Nicole's vulnerable helplessness and the tensions of Dick's relationship with her as both husband and doctor. Dick's story is that of a sensitive and caring man who disintegrates under the strains of a life-style that gnaws away at his moral values and his sense of himself as a man with responsibilities towards society. Fitzgerald wrote in 1933: 'Whether it's something that happened twenty years ago or only yesterday, I must start out with an emotion – one that's close to me and that I can understand ...'[5] Underlying the accurate social detail which is so important to the novel, the emotion which suffuses it is one of sadness for lost hopes and lost dreams in the chaotic and egotistical world of the 1920s.

It is worth noting that Fitzgerald's initial projected title for the novel was *The Drunkard's Holiday*, followed next by *Dr Diver's Holiday*, and that only later did he decide on the phrase from Keats's poem 'Ode to a Nightingale' under which it was published. By implication the earlier titles express rather ironic criticism of Dick Diver, whereas the final choice conveys through language and association a mood and a whole range of feelings concerning time and the transience of happiness and hope. This aspect is discussed further on p. 90.

The reception of the novel

The novel was first published in serial form in *Scribner's Magazine* between January and April 1934. It was then published in April 1934 in the complete version.

To Fitzgerald's keen disappointment, *Tender is the Night* was not particularly well received, either by the critics or by the public, when it came out. He had hoped to repeat his earlier successes. The time-scheme of the novel, which at a first reading may seem complex, appears to have presented problems for some readers, and certainly Fitzgerald diagnosed this as a cause for its lack of popularity. A few years later, when he was trying to persuade his publisher to issue a complete edition of his works, he wrote of the novel: 'Its great fault is that the *true* beginning – the young psychiatrist in Switzerland – is tucked away in the middle of the book.'[6] It seems likely that in making this comment Fitzgerald was trying to find a reason for the lack of public interest rather than expressing his own critical view. He refers, of course, to the fifty-page section in Book II (Chapters I–X, pp. 129–79) which serves as a flashback giving the reader vital information about Dick and Nicole's marriage, information which the young film-star Rosemary Hoyt, through whose eyes they are viewed in Book I, does not possess.

A case in support of Fitzgerald's decision to start the novel at the point in the Divers' life when Dick is beginning to feel he can no longer cope with the situation is put forward throughout this study. Even though Fitzgerald made that comment about the 'true' beginning of the novel, he himself did not actually change it, for there was no new edition of *Tender is the Night* during his life.

The Malcolm Cowley edition

After Fitzgerald's death in 1940, his editor, Malcolm Cowley, reorganized this section of the novel for a new edition, and subsequent readers for many years accepted his version as Fitzgerald's own. Cowley placed the flashback section (Book II, pp. 129–74) at the *beginning* of the novel, calling it Book I and giving it the title 'Case History: 1917–19'. He also divided Fitzgerald's three books into five, each with a title and dates. In his introduction to this new edition Cowley justified these changes on the grounds that Fitzgerald had planned a new edition of the novel this way, and he referred frequently to 'Fitzgerald's new arrangement'. However, it is by no means certain that Fitzgerald did any more than *consider* the possibility of making such a change by jotting ideas in his Notebook. Cowley further sought to justify his own interference with the novel by claiming that he was thus clarifying the issues with which it dealt:

> One fault of the earlier version was its uncertainty of focus. We weren't quite sure in reading it whether the author had intended to write about a whole group of Americans on the Riviera – that is, to make the book a social study with a collective hero – or whether he had intended to write a psychological novel about the glory and decline of Richard Diver as a person.[7]

Cowley suggests that in his new edition 'we are certain' what the novel is about, namely that 'it is a psychological novel, that it is about Dick Diver', but he does not define just how this instant awareness is brought about. Certainly it puts the aspiring young doctor/psychiatrist, Dick Diver, in the forefront of the reader's attention and lets the reader know early on that Nicole is schizophrenic, but this fact emerges all the more poignantly in the original version when the trivialization of Dick's life within a period of six years, 1919–25, has already been so vividly presented in Book I.

Since 1960, new editions of the novel, such as the Penguin edition of 1982, have restored the original version, which is the one used for the purposes of this study.

The First World War and its aftermath in contemporary writing

The Great War of 1914–18 involved the major powers of Europe in four years of devastating battle. The main belligerents were, on the one hand, Imperial Germany and the Austro-Hungarian Empire, and, on the other, France, Italy, Imperial Russia – until the outbreak of internal revolution in 1917 – the British Empire and, ultimately, the United States. Most of the fighting took place on French and Belgian soil; it was characterized by trench warfare, which took a hideous toll of life on both sides (see Dick's comments on p. 67 about 'the dead like a million bloody rugs'), and by new technology, which increased its destructive power: air and submarine warfare was employed in a systematic manner, gas was used in the trenches, the increased mobility of railways meant better transportation, the firing power of guns was greater than ever before.

In 1917 five American ships were sunk. War was declared on Germany, and by October 1918 over one and three-quarter million American troops were in France playing a decisive role in the final offensive which led to Allied victory. It was the first American engagement in Europe in the role of a great power.

The war also accentuated and hastened social, political and economic changes in Central and Eastern Europe, as well as further complicating existing rivalries among the states of Europe. On the outbreak of war in 1914, Sir Edward Grey, British Foreign Secretary, made a remark that anticipated the impact this major conflict was to have on Western civilization: 'The lamps are going out all over Europe; we shall not see them lit again in our lifetime.'

In the novel the presence of many of the Americans travelling in France is associated deliberately with the First World War. Some of the wandering figures seem to have been left in Europe as detritus of the war: ' "You in the army?" "*I'll* say I was. Eighty-fourth Division – ever heard of that outfit?" ' (Book I, p. 105). This young ex-soldier is trying to make his fortune out of American visitors. He is subsisting on the fringes of French life, and turns up again at the end of the novel for the Tour de France, selling American newspapers (Book III, p. 331). Dick himself was originally sent to Europe by his government, although he was too valuable to be posted to the actual front. In the flashback section of Book II, Switzerland, a neutral country, is described as being full of trainloads of the wounded. They too are travelling, uprooted from their own countries:

> Switzerland was an island, washed on one side by the waves of thunder around Gorizia [the Italian front] and on the other by the cataracts [of shells] along the Somme and the Aisne [the Western Front] ... However, no one had missed the long trains of blinded or one-legged men, or dying trunks, that crossed each other between the bright lakes of Constance and Neuchâtel ... As the massacre continued the posters withered away, and no country was more surprised than its sister republic when the United States bungled its way into the war [p. 129].

In the novel, those who linger or have the money to travel in France appear to be lost souls, without a centre of moral identity.

Fitzgerald was not the only American novelist to respond to the implications of American involvement in a destructive conflict of world proportions, whose new technology of gas warfare, tanks and aeroplanes seemed to sweep away many of the older social and moral certainties of life. (In England, young serving soldiers who were also poets, such as Wilfrid Owen, Isaac Rosenberg and Siegfried Sassoon, had already expressed the shock of civilized young men confronting with pain and anger the outrage of trench warfare. The German novelist Erich Maria Remarque had expressed an equally bitter anguish at the affront to human decency in his novel about the trenches, *All Quiet on the Western Front*, which viewed the war from the opposing side.) The American writer who handled the experience of battle most vividly was Ernest Hemingway in his novel *A Farewell to Arms* (1929), set in the campaign in Italy. Hemingway had first-hand knowledge of the war, and, like Fitzgerald, was himself an expatriate in France in the 1920s. His depiction, in *The Sun Also Rises* (1926), of the post-war generation of 'lost' young Americans and Britons wasting their lives in the bars of Paris makes interesting reading beside *Tender is the Night*. Hemingway's characters engage in a frenetic pursuit of excitement and thrills to stop themselves having to face the terror of their own emotional bankruptcy. Some of them have moved beyond the limits of respectable society. Brett, the major woman character, with her emancipated, rather mannish styles of dress and speech, sleeps around, yet she is imprisoned by the fear of her own lack of feeling. The other central figure, Jake, is the only character who achieves any equilibrium in his life, but, significantly, he does so only because he is impotent as a result of a war wound.

For Dick, Nicole and Rosemary in *Tender is the Night*, no such abandonment of personal and sexual morality is possible in the first part of the novel. In Paris in 1925 they are protected by their innocence, which Dick guards in his role of the 'Organizer of private gaiety, curator of a richly incrusted happiness' (Book I, p. 87). There is certainly irony in that final phrase, since their happiness is 'richly incrusted' by Nicole's wealth. By 1929, however, no such moral inhibitions exist. Innocence is no longer of value.

Both these novels make the world war of 1914–18 the historical catalyst in the background of the characters' lives which leaves them without values they can believe in. There is an insistent recurrence of violence in each. Sexual aggressiveness is open in *The Sun Also Rises* and is mirrored in the tactics and organized violence of the bull-ring in the scenes set in Spain; Nicole's violence in *Tender is the Night* grows out of her repressed sexual aggression. Although Hemingway handles physical and sexual aggression more explicitly than Fitzgerald, both novelists relate these, and psychological disturbances as well, to a world which has just passed through a traumatic experience of violence on a scale never before experienced.

In *Tender is the Night* the seemingly glamorous and carefree mood of the early scenes depicting life on the Riviera in the late summer sun gives way to feelings of despair in Dick and mental breakdowns for Nicole. The series of deaths and reminders of death in the Paris scenes is further discussed on pp. 84–5: it is set in motion in the novel by the visit to the trenches which Dick organizes. This day's outing may appear inexplicable in its context of pleasure and parties on the Riviera or in Paris, but it serves to recall the mass destruction that has left its mark on society. As they wander through the trenches near Amiens, Dick is the only one who shows awareness of the implications of that carnage. Abe North had served in the war, but by the summer of 1925 he is incapable of seriousness or imaginative concern. Perhaps Abe feels that Dick is being melodramatic in his sombre allusions to the military strategies, since he makes a game out of them, and says 'consolingly' (Book I, p. 67): 'There are lots of people dead since and we'll all be dead soon.' But Dick's concern is both humane and historical. He views the war as marking the final death-throes of the major European empires, England and France on the one side, Germany on the other:

See that little stream – we could walk to it in two minutes. It took the British a month to walk to it – a whole empire walking very slowly, dying in front and pushing forward behind. And another empire walked very slowly backward a few inches a day, leaving the dead like a million bloody rugs. No Europeans will ever do that again in this generation [p. 67].

In a recent book by Paul Fussell called *The Great War and Modern Memory*, the author comments that the British offensive of 1916 against the Germans, known to the troops as the Great Fuck-Up, was 'the largest engagement fought since the beginnings of civilization'.[8] He gives an account of one attack which was preceded by a week of artillery bombardment, but which ended disastrously when the British soldiers, edging their way forward over a thirteen-mile front, were raked by German machine-guns or trapped on the barbed wire: 'Out of 110,000 who attacked, 60,000 were killed or wounded on this one day ... the record so far. Over 20,000 lay dead between the lines, and it was days before the wounded in No Man's Land had stopped crying out.'[9] Fussell quotes from the autobiography of the poet Edmund Blunden, *The Mind's Eye*, published in 1934, the same year as *Tender is the Night*. Blunden sees this particular attack as marking the end of an era: 'By the end of the day both sides had seen, in a sad scrawl of broken earth and murdered men, the answer to the question. No road. No thorough-fare. Neither race had won, nor could win, the war. The war had won, and would go on winning.'[10] Fussell agrees with this judgement:

> The Great War took place in what was, compared with ours, a static world, where the values appeared stable and where the meanings of abstractions appeared permanent and reliable. Everyone knew what Glory was, and what Honor meant. It was not until eleven years after the war that Hemingway would declare in *A Farewell to Arms* (1929) that 'abstract words such as glory, honor, courage or hallow were obscene beside the concrete names of villages, the number of roads, the names of rivers, the numbers of regiments and the dates.' In the summer of 1914 no one would have understood what he was talking about.[11]

Civilized life was never to be the same again.

What Fussell is tracing is a shift in consciousness during the 1920s as people faced the issues which that period of massive destruction had raised. In the Great War men had shown extraordinary courage – but to what purpose? Abstract words such as 'honour' or 'glory' had been used very freely to raise regiments and send them to a brutal death. The values which language had transmitted were now coming into question. In the visit to the trenches Dick Diver, the most sensitive and morally serious of all the characters, does not so much express that shift in consciousness as mourn the passing of the old, traditional values. The reader is at this stage unable to understand the full personal sense of loss that Dick is voicing ('"All my beautiful lovely safe world blew itself up here with a great gust of high explosive love," Dick mourned persistently' (Book I, p. 68)), but the conversation marks him off from his companions. Nicole is nervous and abstracted; Rosemary is engaged in hero-worshipping Dick and ready to agree with anything he says; Abe North dissociates himself from Dick's seriousness.

Yet there is something slightly incongruous in the presence of these well-heeled and frivolous tourists in this field of the dead, and the final paragraph of the chapter seems to imply this:

> Then, leaving infinitesimal sections of Württembergers, Prussian Guards, chasseurs alpins, Manchester mill hands and Old Etonians to pursue their eternal dissolution under the warm rain, they took the train for Paris. They ate sandwiches of mortadel sausage and bel paese cheese made up in the station restaurant, and drank Beaujolais. Nicole was abstracted, biting her lip restlessly and reading over the guide-books to the battle-field that Dick had brought along – indeed, he had made a quick study of the whole affair, simplifying it always until it bore a faint resemblance to one of his own parties [p. 70].

The last sentence reads somewhat strangely. A 'quick study' is likely to be superficial. Is Dick's rather self-conscious language merely expressing a passing emotion? More likely, Fitzgerald intends it to be incongruous amid such luxury. Indeed, not long before this Rosemary had cast an appraising eye over their expensive and novel beach equipment, and realized the Divers were enjoying 'the first burst of luxury manufacturing after the War', and were the first purchasers (p. 27). The war had not reduced their way of life. This scene therefore has a double significance. Dick's feelings are genuine and to be respected, yet they are undercut by the author's ironic judgement on a way of life devoid of positive values.

The post-war world as wasteland

The image of the wasteland recurs in writing of the post-war period as a potent representation of a society cut adrift from the traditional moral values which once gave life its meaning.

In a deceptively and puzzlingly simple short story by Hemingway called 'Big Two-Hearted River' (1925), the only character is a young man called Nick Adams, who is taking a solitary fishing trip in the Midwest of America. What is characteristic in the story is the restraint of Hemingway's non-committal style, which forces the reader to ponder the significance of what happens. (Fitzgerald's own development of similar narrative techniques is discussed on p. 45.) Nick seems to find emotional peace in the solitude of the open countryside, where he is forced to exercise total self-control in setting up his tent, cooking his food and absorbing himself completely in the habits of the trout he is trying to catch, things which exist outside himself. Yet before he reaches the river and strikes camp he has to make his way over an expanse of black, burnt terrain. No explanation is offered, and the reader is left to determine how far this wasteland symbolizes some traumatic emotional state of Nick's.

The wasteland as a symbol of social and personal sterility and despair occurs elsewhere in the writing of the 1920s. T. S. Eliot's poem *The Waste Land* (1922) offers the most well-known example, a sustained evocation of universal and individual sterility. Eliot draws on Old Testament landscapes of desert, stones and dryness, but builds on these a whole range of images which create a collage of dramas about the pain of being unable to love or to differentiate between experiences. Many of these vignettes of pain and isolation are set in scenes of the contemporary post-war world, though Eliot's concern is not only with this.

Fitzgerald himself, in his 1925 novel *The Great Gatsby*, set in post-war New York during the Prohibition era, employs an expanse of great dustheaps outside the city as a strange and bizarre landscape of decay where grey ghost-figures move about. The Valley of Ashes functions as a symbolic representation of both the lack of feeling in the characters and the materialism of their society. In *The Great Gatsby* it is an image of the greed and carelessness of a sophisticated, wealthy set of characters in whose lives dreams have no place and for whom individuals are as easily disposable as the crates of oranges which arrive on Friday nights in preparation for Gatsby's parties and are carted away as empty skins on Monday mornings. Material values are the only ones that matter: human beings have no value. In *Tender is the Night* the 'great sea of graves' near Amiens which Dick takes his party of friends to visit (Book I, pp. 68–9) is also a wasteland of dead lives. It is a memorial consisting of neat restored trenches and 'great funeral pyres of sorted duds, shells, bombs, grenades, and equipment, helmets, bayonets, gun stocks and rotten leather, abandoned six years in the ground'. It functions in the novel as a reminder of tragically wasted lives. Abe North, Rosemary learns, had once made 'a brilliant and precocious start' as a musician, but 'had composed nothing for seven years' (p. 43), that is, since the war. By 1925 he is a moral derelict who impels himself into a drink-sodden life of chaos and violence, which is to end three or four years later in his being beaten to death in a New York speakeasy (an illegal bar). But Abe is an exception. Most of the characters in the novel remain materially successful even though they are depicted as morally bankrupt.

The prosperous 1920s: a wasteland of wealth

The giant corporations of America (among the earliest of which was the powerful Beef Trust of the Chicago meat-canning industry, significantly made the source of the initial Warren fortune accumulated in Chicago by Nicole's grandfather) were developed during the last quarter of the nineteenth century to control the country's huge capital resources and encourage investment. During the 1920s wealthy and middle-class Americans sank all their money into frantic speculations on the stock market. At the same time great innovations in the techniques of industrial production increased output far beyond the capacity of ordinary Americans to buy, and, because the government imposed high tariffs to prevent other countries gaining a market for their own goods, America found few foreign markets for hers. Over-speculation led to a failure of confidence on the stock market, and by 1929 the prosperous façade of the 1920s had crumbled. Investors everywhere lost their life savings, banks and businesses closed, factories were shut down, and millions of Americans walked the streets looking for work. The effects of the Depression were to last right through the 1930s, leaving an enduring impression on the American consciousness.

Writing to his literary agent about the serialization prospects of *Tender is the Night* in 1933, Fitzgerald stressed: 'It might be wise to accentuate the fact that it does *not* deal with the depression.'[12]

The life-style of the wealthy is deliberately associated in this novel with dereliction and illness, yet it is also glamorous and enviable. Their affluence reflects one aspect of the economic expansion and energy of the 1920s in America. Some critics suggest that Fitzgerald planned the novel to end at a point where the characters would naturally have been oblivious of the financial ruin facing some of them. Tommy Barban's comment near the end concerning his investments that 'All goes well' (Book III, p. 295) would then have a ring of hollow optimism. However, there is no reference to this in the subsequent years covered by the final chapter, and speculation about it is pointless. Fitzgerald's focus on the lives of the very wealthy offers a deliberately selective view of the times. The self-centred, casual exploitation of their power by the wealthy creates its own wasteland of human lives which is characterized by the Swiss clinics and the vulgarized beach of Book III and has its main focus in the wasted life of Dick Diver.

Great wealth is a corrupting force as well as a source of power in the novel. The Warrens are one of the 'the great feudal families' (Book II, p. 142) of the Chicago stockyards and meat-packing factories. When Nicole resumes control of her life in that society at the end of the novel, she admits to Tommy Barban: 'And being well perhaps I've gone back to my true self – I suppose my grandfather was a crook and I'm a crook by heritage, so there we are' (Book III, p. 314). When Rosemary goes shopping with Nicole in Paris, her alert feminine eye notices a difference between the way each of them spends money. Rosemary knows that she has to earn hers, but Nicole spends with the lavish abandon of one to whom the money belongs by right. The authorial voice suspends the narrative to offer an analysis of the meaning of Nicole's financial power. A sustained criticism of the economic system is implicit in the use of words like 'toiled' or 'muscled out':

Nicole was the product of much ingenuity and toil. For her sake trains began their run at Chicago and traversed the round belly of the continent to California; chicle factories fumed and link belts grew link by link in factories; men mixed toothpaste in vats and drew mouthwash out of copper hogsheads; girls canned tomatoes quickly in August or worked rudely at the Five-and-Tens [Woolworths] on Christmas Eve; half-breed Indians toiled on Brazilian coffee plantations and dreamers were muscled out of patent rights in new tractors – these were some of the people who gave a tithe to Nicole, and as the whole system swayed and thundered onward it lent a feverish boom to such processes of hers as wholesale buying, like the flush of a fireman's face holding his post before a spreading blaze [Book I, p. 65].

This passage intrudes so forcefully upon the narrative that it could not possibly be attributed to Rosemary's intelligence, although the initial discrimination is hers. The authorial voice takes over to make a comprehensive indictment of capitalism as a means of exploiting the poor and the helpless internationally. The poor, the masses in both North and South America, are brought into the narrative as the victims of Nicole's lavish requirements. The implications of the final sentence are that retribution must follow. The imagery of fire would seem to indicate revolution, but it is more likely that Fitzgerald, writing after 1930, had in mind the devastating failure of capitalism that caused the Depression rather than a vision of radical political change in the United States.

The presence of the Russians in Cannes in 1925 was a fact of history. The chauffeur who drives Rosemary and her mother on a conducted tour of the Riviera is an émigré nobleman swept out of his country by the Revolution of 1917. He brings to life for the American pair the old resplendent pre-Revolutionary days when other 'big spenders', the Russian princes, spent their fortunes while escaping from the Russian winter. Those 'caviare days' are lost for ever:

Ten years ago [i.e. in 1915], when the season ended in April, the doors of the Orthodox Church were locked, and the sweet champagnes they favored were put away until their return. 'We'll be back next season,' they said, but this was premature, for they were never coming back any more [Book I, p. 24].

The new 'princes' on the European scene are the American millionaires.

23

At a later point in the novel, in Book III, the authorial voice once again intrudes to hold up the narrative. The reader is invited to enter the text and savour the full value of the Divers' entourage as they go to visit their old friend Mary North, now the Contessa di Minghetti. The long paragraph is worth quoting in full.

Regard them, for example, as the train slows up at Boyen where they are to spend a fortnight visiting. The shifting from the wagon-lit has begun at the Italian frontier. The governess's maid and Madame Diver's maid have come up from second class to help with the baggage and the dogs. Mlle Bellois will superintend the hand-luggage, leaving the Sealyhams to one maid and the pair of Pekinese to the other. It is not necessarily poverty of spirit that makes a woman surround herself with life – it can be a superabundance of interest, and, except during her flashes of illness, Nicole was capable of being curator of it all. For example with the great quantity of heavy baggage – presently from the van would be unloaded four wardrobe trunks, a shoe trunk, three hat trunks, and two hat boxes, a chest of servants' trunks, a portable filing-cabinet, a medicine case, a spirit lamp container, a picnic set, four tennis rackets in presses and cases, a phonograph, a typewriter. Distributed among the spaces reserved for family and entourage were two dozen supplementary grips, satchels and packages, each one numbered, down to the tag on the cane case. Thus all of it could be checked up in two minutes on any station platform, some for storage, some for accompaniment from the 'light trip list' or the 'heavy trip list,' constantly revised, and carried on metal-edged plaques in Nicole's purse [Book III, p. 278].

The passage is brilliant in its restraint. What is never openly stated here is that Dick's interior world of idealism and imagination has been buried under the paraphernalia of wealth. His life with Nicole has been deftly cocooned by the whole army of servants whose human presence is revealed only at the end of the novel.

While in Book I, at the Divers' dinner-party, 'the chance apparition of a maid in the background' (p. 37) is referred to as a failure, since it is the duty of domestic staff to be self-effacing in the 'intensely calculated perfection of Villa Diana', in Book III the cook Augustine's eruption in a drunken brawl is chaotic and potentially murderous even though it is handled as comedy by Fitzgerald. She has been drinking their fine wines, but turns the tables on them by insultingly declaring that Dick drinks far more than she (p. 286). What is more, her brother is in the local police and so the wealthy Americans can be flouted. Villa Diana itself is an alien intrusion upon local life, nine small houses having been sacrificed to produce it.

Whereas Nicole merely spends her inheritance, Baby Warren represents an important feature of these vast American fortunes – power. She is perfectly willing to procure Dick's medical services for her sister, and then to cast him off when his job is done: 'That's what he was educated for' (Book III, p. 335). The power the Warrens exercise as their prerogative carries no responsibilities – they are rootless people. Baby Warren uses hers blatantly in the novel. It buys her a position which she enjoys among the old European aristocratic families and insulates her from personal feeling. The power of this kind of wealth is insidious in its effects on Dick. Nicole's free-association monologue exposes the arguments that must have taken place between herself and Dick to break down his resolution to remain independent: 'Why should we penalize ourselves just because there's more Warren money than Diver money' (Book II, p. 176), and 'We must spend my money and have a house – I'm tired of apartments and waiting for you' (p. 178). In Paris Dick's charm discreetly effects an arrangement with the hotel detective to prevent any scandal attaching to Rosemary – and the big luxury hotel – concerning the death of Peterson (Book I, p. 124), but it is backed by his wealth. Some years later in Cannes he is able to buy off the police to prevent criminal charges being brought against the two titled ladies (Book III, pp. 327–8). Within this world the assertive American individual has been cut off from all organic links with family and community. The paradigm of such rootless individuals is the eternal wanderer (cf. the Flying Dutchman), like Dick at the end of the novel.

International travel

The novel is characterized by a pervasive sense of restlessness. Most of the characters are expatriate Americans whose lives are passed in an aimless pursuit of pleasure in Europe. At the social summit are Dick and Nicole Diver and Baby Warren, who are among those described as 'the princely classes in America' (Book I, p. 45); within their orbit are Abe and Mary North and Tommy Barban; forging their way up into their exclusive circles are the McKiskos and Mrs Abrams, to mention only the prominent ones. As a successful film-star, Rosemary Hoyt gains entry into the fashionable world. In Paris, when Dick takes Rosemary to a reception given by a wealthy young American woman who is anxious for an invitation to join his set on the Riviera, Fitzgerald uses incisive language to define the characteristics of the guests. Some of them are tired after 'dissipating all spring and summer'; the others are the 'exploiters' and 'sponges' who are seriously committed to getting something out of them (Book I, p. 83).

The Norths and Baby Warren, in their different ways, travel aimlessly.

Abe North had once been a composer of promise, but at the beginning of the novel he is referred to contemptuously as 'a rotten musician' (Book I, p. 18); and after his death his work is dismissed as of little interest (Book II, p. 218). In Paris his drunken escapades cease to be entertaining to anyone, being nihilistic and destructive. His meaningless death in a New York bar, casually discussed in Dick's hearing in Munich (p. 218), fulfils his tragic death-drive. Baby Warren strenuously denies that she is 'racing around over Europe, chasing one novelty after another, and missing the best things in life' (Book II, p. 236), but the way the narrative focuses on Dick's adverse judgements on her makes it abundantly clear that her 'cold rich insolence' (Book II, p. 195) is a sterile and totally insensitive woman's form of pursuing power. Tommy Barban, who is half American, is a 'hero' and a 'ruler' (Book II, p. 215): '"After all, I am a hero," Tommy said calmly, only half joking' (Book III, p. 291). Fitzgerald seems to imply that his kind of heroism is suspect in the modern world; it involves killing and danger in sorties into Soviet Russia to rescue fugitive aristocrats, or fighting in North Africa against the local tribes, all for doubtful motives: '"Well, I'm a soldier," Barban answered pleasantly. "My business is to kill people. I fought against the Riff because I am a European, and I have fought the Communists because they want to take my property from me"' (Book II, p. 45). In other words, he is very crudely and selfishly motivated in his role of professional adventurer. He also needs the excitement to give meaning to his life.

There is little sense of intimacy among the characters. The narrative concentrates almost wholly on Dick and Nicole Diver's public and social life, which consists of a great deal of travel. The few private, intimate scenes between them emphasize the moments when each is anxiously watching the other for signs of strain or trying to gauge what the other is thinking. Their marriage is represented in the novel largely through scenes of their glamorous life-style: on the beach, at a dinner-party, on the train, in restaurants and hotels, on board a private yacht or in a hairdressing salon. Their life together is also lived publicly in the clinic in the disastrous relationship of husband/wife–doctor/patient.

Like Nicole, Rosemary Hoyt has spent her girlhood in hotel life in France with her mother, and her career as a film-star requires movement from one location to another. The social satellites, such as Mrs Abrams and the McKiskos, who are first seen rather gingerly presenting their bodies to the sun in the opening chapters, are reintroduced later, still climbing socially among the fashionable. They all form a section of the hordes of travelling Americans who bring the coveted dollars to Europe. In 1919, just after the war, Dick is eagerly asked in the Swiss resorts 'if there would be Americans this year' (Book II, p. 163). By the end of the decade the American photographer from Associated Press is ready to catch the fashionable people on the beach for the enjoyment of readers back home (Book III, p. 334), while the Americans in France need to have their *Herald Tribune* or *Sunday Times*, sold at inflated prices, imported from the States (Book II, pp. 105, 218 and III, p. 309). There are 'Two hundred thousand [Americans in Europe] spending ten million [dollars] a summer' (p. 105).

The short chapters of this novel accentuate the sense of restless, rootless lives. The many and varied scenes are filled with brief appearances by unnamed Americans. Some, like the red-haired girl from Knoxville, Tennessee (Book I, p. 69), have made a solitary journey to the 'great sea of graves' that commemorates the dead of the recent war. Others, like the 'gold-star muzzers' (mothers) (Book I, p. 113), have come in organized parties to mourn their dead. The majority of these visitors to Europe, however, have brought their wealth in search of pleasure. 'So the well-to-do Americans poured through the station onto the platforms with frank new faces, intelligent, considerate, thoughtless, thought-for' (p. 95). Like Rosemary and her mother at the beginning of the novel, they are looking for 'high excitement' (p. 12). Yet the presence in the novel of those mourning sisters, wives and mothers, who are briefly glimpsed as they seek the graves of their dead, creates a reminder of carnage amid all the 'fun', and establishes an elegiac note of great import. The feverish pursuit of gaiety is matched by the sombre presence of death. Some of these Americans bring their own form of violence with them from America, and the shabby Jules Peterson who is left dead on Rosemary's bed is a victim of this (Book I, p. 122).

The Jazz Age: universal entertainment for restless people

The 1920s saw the arrival of many of the features of mass entertainment which are familiar today. Commercial radio was set up in 1920, the transatlantic wireless telephone in 1926, and throughout the decade Hollywood was growing into a big industrial enterprise. This was the age of the silent film, and *Daddy's Girl* would belong to that genre, with its over-gesticulatory style of acting, typical of the years before the advent of 'talkies' in 1928 and Al Jolson's appearance in *The Jazz Singer*. Rosemary is the blonde young actress moulded into a star image by the studio publicity machine, which requires her to have an untarnished reputation. In fact, her contract is contingent upon this (Book I, p. 124).

Four years later, towards the end of the decade, she has been allowed to introduce sex appeal into her role in *The Grandeur that was Rome*.

Fitzgerald creates a strong sense of the texture of life in the 1920s by making Rosemary, an outsider figure, first a starlet and then a fully fledged star, one of the images of wish-fulfilment on the screen. In their vast and elaborate expenditure upon the manufacture of dream worlds which both cater for and shape public taste, the film studios create their own wastelands. In Monte Carlo the studio preserves the bizarre debris of recent pictures: 'a decayed street scene in India, a great cardboard whale, a monstrous tree bearing cherries large as basketballs' (Book I, p. 31); while in Rome on location the mock-up of the Forum is larger than the original (Book II, p. 231). Fitzgerald comments of the film company: 'they were risen to a position of prominence in a nation that for a decade had wanted only to be entertained' (p. 232).

The recurrent use of popular music in the novel contributes both a sense of the decade and also serves to heighten the emotional content of scenes. When Dick, now obsessed by his passion for Rosemary in the Paris scenes of Book I, telephones her just for the sake of hearing her voice, he still cannot obliterate from his mind Collis Clay's gossip about Rosemary engaging in some heavy love-making with a student the year before (she is, after all, 'nearly complete' (Book I, p. 12)). As Dick embarks on a rather banal and unsatisfactory conversation with her over the phone (Book I, pp. 106–7), he hears in the background 'little gusts of music [that] wailed around her –

> "And two – for tea.
> And me for you,
> And you for me
> Alow-own."'

This popular song is used to effect an ironic contrast between the feelings of Dick and Rosemary. At one end of the phone he desires her, but at the other she immediately resumes her childish letter to her mother about her latest infatuation ('Of course I Do Love Dick Best but you know what I mean'). 'Me for you and you for me' has no place in their lives.

Popular music pervades *Tender is the Night*, whether from phonographs (record players), radios or dance bands. Dick at one point sits down to the piano to play the tune running through his head, 'Tea for Two', but daren't in case he should upset Nicole by reminding her of Rosemary (Book II, p. 187). The songs are used in the novel as something essentially American, a feature of American life and American entertainment which has been imported into France. In addition to this, the banal lyrics function in particular scenes to underscore all the things the characters know or guess or feel but never talk to each other about. Fitzgerald thus catches the tone of the age, but also uses the snatches of music to give an emotional significance to a scene which may be lyrical in quality or may be ironic.

One of the flashback scenes at the beginning of Book II, which takes place before the start of the Jazz Age proper, is a good example of the way a mood of tenderness and excitement is enhanced by tunes. In 1918 (Chapter V) Nicole Warren invites Dick Diver to listen to some hit records sent over from America. Dick is not really interested in them, but he is fascinated by the way this waif of a patient becomes excited and confident as she talks about such tunes as 'Hindustan', 'Why Do They Call Them Babies?', 'I'm Glad I Can Make You Cry', 'Wait Till the Cows Come Home' and 'Good-by, Alexander' (pp. 150–51). Just talking about them and dreaming of dancing to them brings Nicole to life and restores her, momentarily, to the beautiful young girl she is, and Dick is touched *and* excited. The next time they meet it is also a moonlit night, and Nicole, half deliberately, half innocently, makes a profound effect on this handsome young doctor who, at twenty-six to her eighteen, is sexually attractive to her and yet also has the authority of a father-figure. She waits for him in the moonlight and takes him to a quiet corner of the grounds 'facing miles and miles of rolling night' to listen to her records (p. 151):

> They were in America now ... They were so sorry, dear; they went down to meet each other in a taxi, honey; they had preferences in smiles and had met in Hindustan, and shortly afterward they must have quarrelled, for nobody knew and nobody seemed to care – yet finally one of them had gone and left the other crying, only to feel blue, to feel sad.

By the restraint of his style, Fitzgerald conveys the emotions Dick and Nicole are experiencing beneath the conscious act of listening to the music. For Dick, the moonlight enhances the magic of Nicole's effect upon him as they respond sensuously to the combination of 'the thin tunes' and the moonlit solitude. Their emotions are highly sexual, yet they are also innocent and tender. The novel is subtitled *A Romance,* and this scene contributes to the romantic feeling which is important in the first half of the novel.

Yet Fitzgerald adds an ironic touch before this chapter ends, though the irony may not be apparent to the reader until later in the novel. Nicole sings to Dick:

> 'Lay a silver dollar
> On the ground

> And watch it roll
> Because it's round –'

She seems to bring with her 'the essence of a continent' (p. 152); she reminds him of their distant homeland, America. The silver dollar is, however, also a reminder of her vast American fortune.

Later in Montreux Dick watches Nicole dancing to the tune 'Poor Butterfly' (p. 168), and the application of these words to her is so obvious as to make him think of her secret. Years later, when their marriage is under severe strain and they are together in the Lausanne hotel, there is a flare-up between them when, for the first time, Dick makes a bitter reference to her mental illness (Book III, p. 272). They sit together in the bar while someone plays a record of 'The Wedding of the Painted Doll' and again the relation of the title to Nicole is significant. Months later, when they are back on the Riviera, Nicole sings as Dick plays some new jazz from America on the piano (p. 311):

> 'Thank y' father-r
> Thank y' mother-r
> Thanks for meetingup with one another –'

Dick is ready to go on protecting Nicole from all associations which might upset her, but Nicole exclaims: 'Oh, play it! ... Am I going through the rest of life flinching at the word "father"?' Neither of them says any more on the matter, and Fitzgerald offers no comment on Nicole's recovery to health. He leaves it to the reader to grasp the implications that Nicole is no longer dependent on Dick. The song fills a gap between the two where there would otherwise be silence: they have nothing to say to each other: 'It was lonely and sad to be so empty-hearted toward each other' (p. 312). At such moments the novel demands an awareness of the contemporary developments in psychology and psychoanalysis, particularly the Oedipal complex.

Developments in modern psychology

The psychoanalytic movement developed in the early years of the twentieth century, and by the time of the First World War and the early 1920s was established on an international scale. The pioneer figure was Sigmund Freud (1856–1939), working in Vienna, and others were Carl Gustav Jung (1875–1961) in Switzerland and John Dewey (1859–1952) in Chicago. In *Tender is the Night*, young Dr Diver's early training and study take him to two of these centres, Vienna and Switzerland. Freud made important theoretical contributions to the understanding of the unconscious element of the human personality throughout his life, but some of his early insights were most influential. He stressed the importance of infant sexual development in determining the adult personality and named one stage of this the Oedipus complex, when the young child is attracted to the parent of the opposite sex and wants to displace the other parent, the aggressive impulses resulting from this being resolved by identification with the parent of the same sex. He also stressed the importance of the unconscious mind and its role in repressing or suppressing whatever is unpleasant to the individual as a form of defence. One of Freud's most important psychoanalytic techniques was the use of free association during treatment. Patients were encouraged to relax on a couch and to say whatever came into their minds. Another technique was the interpretation of dreams, since Freud saw in these a rich source of emotionally significant ideas.

In addition to the travelling Americans pursuing their grief or their pleasure in Europe, there is a third group in the Swiss mental clinics. Rich persons' clinics, as Franz calls them (Book II, p. 133), they may be, but beneath their aura of wealth Fitzgerald creates disturbing images of human derelicts. When Dick Diver recounts to Franz his meeting with the young patient Nicole Warren in the grounds of the clinic, he calls her 'a beautiful shell' (p. 134). Professor Dohmler's 'plant' (a rather strange use of a word customarily denoting a factory), at its founding the first modern clinic for treating mental illness, is described in the following terms: 'at a casual glance no layman would recognize it as a refuge for the broken, the incomplete, the menacing, of this world, though two buildings were surrounded with vine-softened walls of a deceptive height' (p. 135). The words 'broken', 'incomplete', 'menacing' are made shocking by their impersonality, yet they convey both the pathos and the horror of shattered lives. At one point in Dick's growing relationship with Nicole he finds himself watching a beret which turns out not to be Nicole's but that of 'a skull recently operated on. Beneath it human eyes peered' (p. 160). The inmates of the clinic which Dick and Franz run in partnership from 1926 to 1929 are associated very deliberately with moral degeneracy or dereliction. The whole tenor of emotions in the novel moves from innocence, tenderness, victimization and helplessness in the early section to egotism and even viciousness in the later one, and the mental cases mirror this shift. While in the first clinic they are represented as victims, similar to the victims of war, in the second clinic they are decadent and degenerate, the products of a grossly materialist society at the end of the 1920s.

The most interesting of his patients in the second clinic, as far as Dick

31

is concerned, is the American woman painter whose body has become 'a living agonizing sore' and her existence a 'sleepless torture' (Book II, p. 202). She terms herself 'a ghostly echo from a broken wall' (p. 203). Dick can offer her no help other than kindness, yet he feels an identification with her which is given significance at the end of the novel when he too seems to fade like 'a ghostly echo from a broken wall'. Franz later asserts, after her death, that the cause was syphilis, a sexually transmitted disease, and Dick wearily lets the subject rest there. The novel thus leaves open-ended the matter of her disease.

One of Dick's last patients, whom he goes to Lausanne to interview, is a young Chilean homosexual who is regarded by his father as corrupt. Another guest in the Lausanne hotel is the sick and dying Devereux Warren, Nicole's self-indulgent father, who, even though he is apparently near to death, is another travelling American, always on the move. In the same international resort hotel are

> rich ruins, fugitives from justice, claimants to the thrones of mediatized principal-ities, [who] lived on the derivatives of opium or barbitol listening eternally as to an inescapable radio, to the coarse melodies of old sins. This corner of Europe does not so much draw people as accept them without inconvenient questions. Routes cross here – people bound for private sanitariums or tuberculosis resorts in the mountains, people who are no longer persona grata in France or Italy [Book III, p. 268].

Where the routes of the wounded crossed during the war, now the trains bear the outcast and degenerate products of the 1920s. The reintroduction of Devereux Warren at this point in the narrative is significant. A wreck of a man, an alcoholic, he once again evades confrontation with his own moral carelessness and self-indulgence by moving out of the hotel (p. 271).

Dick's final patient in the clinic is a young alcoholic, but by this time Dick's own drinking is evident to his patients. The revelation of this fact comes as a deliberately contrived shock to the reader:

> He drank claret with each meal, took a night-cap, generally in the form of hot rum, and sometimes he tippled with gin in the afternoons – gin was the most difficult to detect on the breath. He was averaging a half-pint of alcohol a day, too much for his system to burn up [p. 274].

Shortly before this revelation, a complaint that he has kissed a young girl, the daughter of one of the patients, also reflects on Dick's integrity as a doctor, making a contrast with his early relationship with the young patient Nicole Warren in the first clinic. Whereas that relationship was poignant and tender, this casual kiss is one which he has since forgotten about (Book II, p. 205). Dick has deteriorated as a person during the 1920s.

Given that *Tender is the Night* so imaginatively and successfully blends the contemporary consciousness into a taut, beautifully controlled narrative with an interesting theme, why was it not popularly received?

2. The Time-scheme of the Novel

Chapter 1 posed the question of the relative failure of *Tender is the Night* when it first appeared. Fitzgerald's own answer to this question in terms of the time-scheme of the novel has already been referred to (see p. 14). Over the years other criticisms have been levelled at some of the ways in which Fitzgerald handled the actual period of time covered by the action. We will examine these two areas of difficulty first.

The diagrammatic representation on p. 35 of the time-scheme makes clear how selectively Fitzgerald handled time. Book I, for instance, covers just one to two months in 1925, while in Book II four pages of text span the six years after Dick and Nicole's marriage and also briefly bring the narrative back to Rosemary's first day on the beach in 1925 which opened the novel. At the end of her free-association monologue Nicole comments on 'that girl' (Book II, p. 179): the reader has to assume that she is replying to some other character – Abe or Mary North, perhaps – who has recognized the young star of *Daddy's Girl*. Her further comment, 'Well, we're getting very fashionable for July – seems very peculiar to me,' acts as a reminder for the reader of those intruding newcomers on the beach at the beginning of the novel, Mrs Abrams and Co., who are changing the intimate character of the beach created by the Divers. The action then moves forward again to August 1925, when the Divers have returned to their villa to allow Nicole to recuperate after her devastating bout of illness in Paris at the end of Book I, pp. 125–6.

A brief summary of events in the order of narration reveals how the action is accelerated in the second half of Book II and in Book III. The fact that there is no reference to actual dates compounds the problem of understanding the time-scheme in these two books.

A summary of events in the order of narration

Book I, pp. 11–126: summer 1925

I–XI   While taking what is intended to be a short holiday on the Riviera, the young American film-star Rosemary Hoyt makes the acquaintance of the wealthy Divers and their friends, Abe and Mary North and Tommy Barban. She is

The time-scheme of *Tender is the Night*

Book I	Book II				Book III
pp. 11–126	*pp. 129–175*	*pp. 175–9*	*pp. 179–197*	*pp. 198–256*	*pp. 259–338*
Summer 1925 (June/July)	Flashback to 1917–19, when Dick first met Nicole	1919–25	August/November/December 1925 pick up where Book I ended with the Divers' return to Cannes after Nicole's illness in Paris	1928 (?)	Spring/summer 1929 (?)
1. On the Riviera	1. In Dr Dohmler's Swiss clinic	Nicole's free-association interior monologue	1. In Cannes	1. In the Swiss mental clinic	1. In the Swiss clinic
2. In Paris	2. In Montreux on holiday		2. In Gstaad on a skiing holiday	2. In Munich	In Lausanne
				3. In Rome	3. Travelling
					4. On the Riviera

almost eighteen, Dick Diver is thirty-four and Nicole Diver is twenty-four. She falls in love with Dick and with the glamour of their lives.

XII–XXV   She goes with them on a trip to Paris, and is initiated into a world of luxury and fun.

XIII   They visit one of the First World War battlefields and only Dick is moved to grief.

XIX   When they go to the station to see off Abe North on the boat-train taking him on the first stage of his trip home to New York, where he is to resume his musical career, a man is shot dead before their eyes. This brings to the surface certain tensions among them.

XX   Dick succumbs to an affair with Rosemary and begins to feel infatuated with her, but he is inwardly disturbed by the sense that he is losing control of his life.

XXII–XXV   Abe North, who couldn't bring himself to leave Paris, returns on a drunken spree. He sets off a chain of events which ends in the grotesque death of Peterson in Rosemary's hotel room. Nicole has a mental breakdown as a result of the murders and the strain of knowing of Dick's affair.

Book II, pp. 129–256: 1917–19, 1919–25, 1925 and 1928 (?)

I–X
*A flash-
back*   These ten chapters are in the form of a flashback to 1917–19 in Switzerland, when Dick Diver, a young officer in the US army, has just been demobbed and is considering his career as a psychiatrist.

I   The first chapter sketches Dick's intellectual ability and aspirations but points out his emotional immaturity and lack of judgement.

II   In 1919 Dick and his fellow psychiatrist, Franz, discuss a young American patient staying at the clinic where Franz works.

III   Franz gives an account of Nicole's arrival about eighteen months earlier at the age of sixteen. He recounts how Dr Dohmler had elicited with difficulty from her American millionaire father the story of a brief incestuous relationship he had had with his young daughter and of how this had led to her breakdown.

V–VII Nicole's 'transference' of feeling to Dick fills him with pity and at the same time enchants him. Franz warns him that he should not allow himself to become personally involved with her.

VIII–X Dick takes a holiday in Montreux and meets Nicole, newly discharged from the clinic. She establishes a hold over his feelings and he finds himself engaged. Nicole's elder sister, Baby Warren, had wanted to enlist the services of a doctor for her. Dick will now be her doctor as well as her husband.

X (pp. 175–9) Nicole's seemingly rambling free-association monologue
1919–25 covers the period of their lives from 1919 to 1925. It is clear to the reader that she has been very seriously ill and that Dick's life has been devoted to caring for her. It is also clear that her wealth has figured increasingly in their lives.

XI–XII In August 1925, after the trip to Paris, Nicole's breakdown
Late requires a return to the Riviera. The party has broken up
1925 and Dick makes a token effort to resume work on his book on psychiatry.

XIII During Christmas 1925 they take a skiing holiday in Gstaad, Switzerland, with Baby Warren. Franz arrives and proposes that Dick go into partnership with him in a clinic, using Nicole's immense wealth to buy it. Baby Warren asserts her power by supporting the proposal as an investment. Dick resents this.

XIV Two to three years have passed. In the clinic Dick reflects
1928(?) that he is now thirty-eight, a middle-aged man. He feels he is owned by Nicole's wealth.

XV Nicole has another, violent, breakdown in which she tries to kill herself, Dick and their two young children by steering their car over the mountain.

37

XVI–XVIII Dick takes a holiday by himself to recover from the crisis. In Munich he hears that Abe North has been murdered in New York, and he reflects bitterly on his own life, wasted in trying to teach the rich the elements of decency. News of his father's death reaches him, causing him to reflect even more on his own moral values. He returns to America for the funeral.

XIX–XXIII Back in Europe, Dick goes to Rome and meets Rosemary Hoyt, who is working on a film. They resume their former affair, but neither finds any pleasure in it. Dick gets drunk and is beaten up by the police. Baby Warren, who is also there, uses her social influence to get him out of prison, and now feels that she has a moral hold over him. Dick feels marked for life by shame and guilt.

Book III, pp. 259–338: spring and summer 1929 (?)

I–III Franz begins to regard Dick as a failure in the clinic and Dick is increasingly aware of his own lack of interest in the work. His alcoholism is now evident, and when Franz finds another backer for the clinic he eases Dick out of the partnership. Dick is relieved at the change in his life.

IV The Divers, with their son of eleven and daughter of nine, visit their old friend Mary North, now the Contessa di Minghetti and living in style. The visit is disastrous, as Dick, unlike his old self, seems to arouse hostility wherever he goes.

V Back on the Riviera, the Divers meet their old friend Tommy Barban, who makes no attempt to conceal his attraction for Nicole once he senses that there are tensions between them. Dick, who is now drinking heavily, courts further humiliation and hostility, this time at the hands of a decadent English woman, Lady Caroline Sibly-Biers.

VI–VIII Nicole, very aware of Tommy Barban's sexual attractiveness, feels confident enough to begin an affair with him. She wants to revel in her own sexual power with the freedom she sees other women enjoying. She is now twenty-nine and ready for a life without Dick and without the constraints of his moral world. On the beach, Dick is ignored by Mary Minghetti and makes a fool of himself

	while trying to impress Rosemary Hoyt, who is holding court there. Nicole cannot bear to watch him.
IX	Dick and Nicole are now unable to communicate with each other at any depth or level of honesty. Nicole knows that he is suffering, but she completes her transference to Tommy Barban, rejecting Dick's values. Dick has been silently encouraging her to make the break and free herself from his influence. He is now free.
X	Dick resumes his old moral authority when he obtains the release from prison of Mary Minghetti and Lady Caroline Sibly-Biers, who were there on rather distasteful sex offences.
XI	The Divers arrange their separation without rancour or violence. Dick's authority still has enough weight to achieve that.
XII–XIII	Dick quietly bids farewell to his beach, where he is now an alien figure among the fashionable. He becomes only a memory in Nicole's mind as she traces his progress in America through smaller and smaller towns.

The period of time covered by the novel

Early criticism of the organization of the time in the novel has already been mentioned. There has also been criticism of the way Fitzgerald handles the period of time dealt with in Books II and III.

Fitzgerald took great care to work out important dates in his characters' lives in his Notebook.[1] The actual span of time covered is from June 1925 in Book I to (probably) summer 1929 in Book III, with the flashback to 1917–19 in Book II. Critics have pointed out that references to the passing of time in Book II are not very clear, once Dick and Franz have entered into partnership in the clinic. At the beginning of Chapter XIV, Book II, Dick reflects on 'this past year and a half' in the clinic, and that he is thirty-eight years old, but no year is mentioned. Nicole is referred to in the final chapters of Book III as twenty-nine years old. This would appear to bring the action up to 1930, although Fitzgerald's Notebook entries clearly give the date of the final events as 1929. This may seem a point of minor importance, but critics have puzzled over the question from opposing points of view. There are those who say that Dick Diver's deterioration happens too quickly to be credible, and that therefore 1930 would be a more realistic year. Others argue that the novel reflects the economic prosperity of Americans so accurately that if it ended in 1930 it would have to take account of the Wall Street Crash of late 1929 which put an end to the boom years and heralded the Depression and its devastating effect on Americans (see p. 22). Yet in the final chapters Tommy Barban states emphatically that his stocks are doing nicely (Book III, p. 295), and the lives of the wealthy set on the beach appear to be untouched by the menace of financial disaster. On the grounds that this last point is a good one, the year 1929 is accepted in this critical study as being correct. As for the speed of Dick Diver's deterioration, the evidence in the novel suggests that Fitzgerald intended this to be a rapid process, once the cracks in his façade had become obvious to *himself* during those moments in Paris in Book I. The summer of 1925, on which Fitzgerald lavishes so much care and imagination in that first book – or 'introduction', as he called it in a letter – is therefore the key period in the novel, and as such is clearly defined.

In addition to finding difficulties in grasping the time-scheme of the novel, early readers may have failed to appreciate some qualities in Fitzgerald's presentation of the narrative which are directly related to the organization of time. Book I is the real crux of the matter, representing as it does those few weeks in June/July 1925 which chronologically belong in the middle of the twelve-year span of the novel and yet are isolated from it. It therefore stands in problematic relation to Book II, being linked to the end of Nicole's free-association monologue by Rosemary's appearance as a stranger on the beach in June (p. 179), and also leading directly on to August when the action is resumed in Cannes after Nicole's devastating outbreak of illness at the end of Book I.

Book I as the crux of the time-scheme

The full artistic significance of what Fitzgerald achieved by detaching Book I from its chronological sequence is discussed in Chapter 5 in the context of narrative structure. However, the fact that the summer of 1925 represents a watershed in Dick's emotional life is expressed by features of the style and organization of Book I which seem to be intended to puzzle and disturb the reader. Some of these will now be discussed in terms of the use of shifting points of view and the role of the authorial voice, Fitzgerald's creation of different levels of interest through his handling of details, and the seeming disjunction between scenes in Book I.

The use of shifting points of view and the role of the authorial voice

The narration of Book I focuses on three points of view: first that of Rosemary, appraising glamorous strangers and their novel way of life; then very briefly that of Nicole (pp. 34–7), pondering Dick's motivation; then finally that of Dick in Paris, though it ends with Rosemary's horrified understanding of the meaning of those terrible screams coming from Nicole's bathroom (p. 126) which forms the climax of Book I. The artistic significance of this patterning of viewpoints is discussed in Chapter 5 (pp. 82, 97–101).

Rosemary is young and naïve, though she is quite capable of making social discriminations about the two groups on the beach, the exclusive little set which belongs and the social climbers who do not (p. 14). Yet even Rosemary, who after all is an actress and a thoroughly calculating girl, is not too naïve to realize that Dick is putting on a performance: 'After a while she realized that the man in the jockey cap was giving a quiet little performance for this group' (pp. 14–15); 'Oh, we're such *actors*—you and I' (p. 118), she tells Dick in Paris. She never stops to consider why this should be so, but the sudden switches to other points of view or the intrusive comments by the authorial voice encourage the reader to do so. Fitzgerald's technique engages the reader's interest in the psychology of the characters. The suggestion was made in Chapter 1 that he was utilizing the techniques of the new science of psychoanalysis in the novel by gradually revealing the psychological truths beneath surface appearances. By allowing different characters to watch and analyse and comment on each other he draws the reader into the process too. Nicole's analysis of Dick (pp. 36–7) provides the reader with a key to his charm: 'He won everyone quickly with an exquisite consideration and a politeness that moved so fast and intuitively that it could be examined only in its effect.' It also provides the reader with the means of understanding the element of calculation in Dick's encounters with bank clerks (p. 102) or with the hotel detective (p. 124).

Although there are these three shifting viewpoints with their different levels of understanding, Dick Diver remains the figure of central interest, since both Rosemary and Nicole exist in the novel in relation to him. Fitzgerald establishes early in Book I Dick's personal magnetism: everyone, not only an impressionable young woman like Rosemary, succumbs to his charm, which is expressed through his courtesy and code of manners. But Dick himself remains a puzzling figure to the reader. When his consciousness becomes the centre of the action his self-awareness is important in making the reader perceive a gulf between the surface glamour and the reality of his inner self. He acknowledges to himself 'the grinding activity of his mind' (p. 111); he is aware of his own increasing hesitations and uncertainties; he is ashamed of the power of his wealth which requires his shirtmaker or his tailor to fuss over him in shifting 'an inch of silk on his arm' (p. 117); he feels himself driven mad by his own chaotic impulses, 'demoniac and frightened, the passions of many men inside him and nothing simple that he could see' (p. 117).

In addition to the three points of view from which the action is narrated, Fitzgerald himself enters the narrative as author; he uses his own voice to direct the reader's attention to the characters, but of course it is an impersonal voice rather than his own, since he is commenting on fictions. The role of this authorial voice is important in the novel, but particularly so in relation to the organization of the time-scheme, which places the summer of 1925 at the beginning; it undercuts Rosemary's simple view of the Divers in 1925 by pointing out, for instance, that 'the nursery-like peace and good will' of their life on the beach is 'part of a desperate bargain with the gods and had been attained through struggles she could not have guessed at', and that 'a qualitative change had already set in' (p. 30).

A close critical reading of one particular paragraph in Book I will show that Fitzgerald is preparing the reader for an understanding of Dick's inner tension and growing despair. To his friends and acquaintances Dick is the personification of the gentleman, but the authorial voice holds up the action to analyse him for the reader. This occurs at a point when, during their stay in Paris, Dick is beginning to be obsessed by his attraction towards Rosemary, and is particularly troubled by the gossip passed on by Collis Clay of her love-making session the previous year on a train with an undergraduate (p. 100). He begins to behave quite uncharacteristically, even hanging around her studio in the hope of seeing her. He knows that he has reached a turning point in his life,

a turning point ... out of line with everything that had preceded it – even out of line with what effect he might hope to produce upon Rosemary. Rosemary saw him always as a model of correctness – his presence walking around this block was an intrusion. But Dick's necessity of behaving as he did was a projection of some submerged reality: he was compelled to walk there, or stand there, his shirt-sleeve fitting his wrist and his coat sleeve encasing his shirt-sleeve like a sleeve valve, his collar molded plastically to his neck, his red hair cut exactly, his hand holding his small briefcase like a dandy ... Dick was paying some tribute to things unforgotten, unshriven, unexpurgated [pp. 103–4].

Clearly, a contrast is being offered between the exterior man with his 'fine glowing surface' (p. 94) and his tormented inner self. To the world Dick presents the model of a wealthy gentleman: he is a product of superb tailoring, good barbering and fine accessories. At this point the authorial voice employs two different sets of images to portray Dick's state of mind, which is still, as yet, largely unknown to the reader. Just before this passage the comment is made that, despite his dignity, Dick is 'swayed and driven as an animal' (p. 103) by his passion for Rosemary; in the paragraph itself imagery with strong religious overtones is used: 'Dick was paying some tribute to things unforgotten, unshriven, unexpurgated.' 'Unshriven' means without having confessed one's sins and done penance for them; 'unexpurgated' means without having achieved purification. The metaphorical significance of these terms is that Dick is suppressing a deep sense of his own guilt and that he is doing so at a cost which will have to be paid one day. Dick's new passion for Rosemary is connected with his self-doubt and torment, even though he knows that she will never understand his feelings.

Dick's isolation at this point and his sense of having reached a crisis in his life are intensified by the description of the sombre notices in the nearby shop-window advertising funerals. The reader may feel that the language of death and guilt is too insistent: it implies the moral seriousness of Dick's 'submerged reality' without providing sufficient access to his inner world. Yet this moment in the narrative alerts the reader to the strains beneath the veneer of charm and total control with which Dick confronts his society. It also intensifies the humiliating experience of his passion for Rosemary, who is shown in the next chapter to be luxuriating in her capacity to arouse feeling in a sexually attractive, successful older man. By now the narrative is firmly focused on Dick Diver, and by returning in the flashback sequence of Book II to Dick's hopeful young manhood, Fitzgerald gives the reader the double perspective which is so tragic in its implications. The probing comments by the authorial voice alert the reader to Dick's moral crisis and also make reading the novel a complex process of following hints and clues.

The creation of different levels of interest through the handling of details

Fitzgerald is often accused of being too attracted to the world of wealth and of depicting it too glamorously. In Book I the sheer delight of a wealthy life-style which carries enormous power is evident in even the single detail of those 'deferential' palm-trees in the opening paragraph. All the details of clothes, the discreetly invisible servants, cars, trend-setting beachwear and equipment, not to mention luxury hotels, which characterize the Divers' style of living contribute considerable narrative interest in the way they are made an integral part of the characters' own moods. The intensity of feeling generated in a number of the scenes arises out of the glamour with which Dick manages to invest their way of life and out of the beautiful settings to which their wealth gives these characters access. In this novel, as in all Fitzgerald's work, lyrical intensity of feeling is thus inextricably connected with wealth. The dinner-party at the Villa Diana is an example of this (p. 37), as is the exhilaration of the early morning in Paris at the end of Dick's night of revelry, even though he has left the party by then (p. 91). Yet there is an ambivalence about these scenes, particularly the dinner-party with its bizarre epilogue, which puzzles the reader.

Fitzgerald handles the scenes in the novel on two levels of interest. There is the interest of the surface values of characters' lives and relationships, which is heightened by the focus given by particular angles of perception – that of Rosemary, Dick or Nicole. At a first reading this may appear to be the primary interest, particularly in Book I. But underlying these scenes, and giving them significance in the novel, is the real drama – that taking place within the consciousness of Dick Diver. For instance, in Book I the initial glamour of the Divers' lives is enhanced by touches of comic contrast with the habits and personalities of the newcomers on the beach, Mrs Abrams, the McKiskos, etc. The latter are rather inept on the beach compared with the habitués who set the tone of beach life – the Divers. Mr McKisko's style of swimming becomes a source of ironic comedy in the contrast it makes with the grace and apparent ease of the sophisticated group as he flings himself into the shallows with a 'stiff-armed batting of the Mediterranean' and looks round 'with an expression of surprise that he was still in sight of the shore' (p. 17). But Dick's decision to invite these incompatible and enviously hostile people to a party 'where there's a brawl and seductions' (p. 36) is puzzling and causes Nicole to ponder on his need to generate intense excitement around himself. Her questioning mind in turn requires the reader to understand that the chief focus of interest lies in the private, carefully guarded inner world of Dick Diver. Dick's own confession to Rosemary that he invited these guests because he wants the summer 'to die violently' (p. 47) focuses the psychological interest on him and puts the opening series of Riviera scenes into a new perspective.

To give another example, in the Paris scenes of Book I, the narrative interest seems to concentrate on the surface details of Dick's affair with Rosemary. Rosemary obviously enjoys playing her role in this, but Fitzgerald's skilful use of detail makes it clear that this facile girl is widening her experience of sexuality at the expense of Dick's feelings. On one occasion, after she has played a star scene in her hotel bedroom and Dick has gently refused to make love to her, she sinks back on the bed:

When the door closed she got up and went to the mirror, where she began brushing her hair, sniffling a little. One hundred and fifty strokes Rosemary gave it, as usual, then a hundred and fifty more. She brushed it until her arm ached, then she changed arms and went on brushing [p. 77].

The detail related here says a great deal about Rosemary, and the lack of any real emotional involvement on her part, in the way it creates a clear visual image of her routine beauty care. Her looks are her livelihood – and these come first. Dick is being drawn into an emotional entanglement with a very shallow girl who is planning an enjoyable game at his expense.

As Book II picks up the thread of the time sequence in August 1925 (p. 179), the emphasis is placed on Dick's sense of the waste and trivialization of his life and on his trapped position. But in Book I there is no such single focus: the narrative both offers a glittering reflection of the lives of the pleasure-seeking rich, with details of clothes, hairstyles, purchases in fashionable shops, night life and travel presenting a profusion of narrative interest, and also requires the reader to probe into the signs of psychological, moral and emotional tension in the lives of the Divers. Therefore there seems to be little sequential narration in the normal sense.

The seeming disjunction between scenes in Book I

Although Fitzgerald looked towards Hollywood as a source of income or employment, he was also fascinated by film as an art form: in 1930 he commented that the 'talkies' would put even the best novelists out of business. He actually worked briefly in Hollywood in 1927, in the middle of writing *Tender is the Night*, in order to tide himself over financially and to gain inside experience of studio life. Perhaps this initial acquaintance with the film studios gave him knowledge of the cutting that goes on in a projection room. He certainly utilized his later acquaintance with the film world as material for his final, unfinished novel set in Hollywood, *The Last Tycoon*.

In a film there is usually no narrating voice to make connecting links between events, and the locations or time sequences may shift constantly; there is seldom a narrator to explain or define characters' psychology or actions: the story *seems* to tell itself through camera shots, the use of significant details or strong dialogue. It is possible that in *Tender is the Night* Fitzgerald was employing some of the techniques of this new art form. In the Paris episode, for example, a whole sequence of short scenes involving different settings and characters, some of whom are named, but most of whom remain anonymous strangers glimpsed in particular attitudes, forms a background to the lives of the Divers. After impinging on the group's consciousness, these strangers vanish totally. Maria Wallis shoots the Englishman about to leave on the boat-train (p. 95), but no explanation is ever offered. This constant movement conveys the restlessness of the 1920s and of the group too. The sudden changes in scene and mood create a sense of concealed tension and nerves increasingly on edge, but it is left to the reader to respond to the psychological implications.

The same is true of the visit to the battlefield of the 1914–18 war discussed on p. 18. It is a puzzling episode, which seems to be out of place. Dick's comment about 'All my lovely safe world' (p. 68) being blown to smithereens in the trenches may seem overly self-conscious in the context of the holiday mood of their visit to Paris, and the judgement by the authorial voice that Dick 'mourned persistently' may confirm that he is being over-dramatic, but the reader is disturbed by this intrusion of reminders of death.

Constantly in Book I the reader is required to fit together the moods generated in many seemingly unrelated incidents. What is clear, however, is that these incidents serve to place the focus on Dick as a complex personality beneath his veneer of charm and ease. Moreover, by using the naïve newcomer, Rosemary Hoyt, enjoying the pleasures and power of wealth for the first time, as the catalyst who releases Dick's pent-up feelings through her youth and magnetism, Fitzgerald creates a level of real narrative interest. He uses it as a means of indirectly revealing Dick's emotional and moral sense of himself in crisis at a point midway in the time-span of the novel. The summer of 1925 is thus brought into dramatic focus as the key point of psychological interest in the narrative.

3. Dick Diver

'The Crack-Up'

A selection of Fitzgerald's short stories and autobiographical essays published under the title *The Crack-Up with Other Pieces and Stories* (Penguin Books, 1965) offers an interesting range of other work written during those nine years when *Tender is the Night* was taking shape. Although this collection covers a period of sixteen years, 1924–40, almost all the pieces share a certain feature: memory at work, recalling, assessing, reliving a successful past. The past in question is a time of youth, the Great War, the heyday of silent films, the hectic age of the 1920s to which Fitzgerald gave the memorable title the Jazz Age. In one essay, 'Echoes of the Jazz Age', first published in 1931, during the early stages of the Depression, Fitzgerald writes of the horror of looking back on a wasted youth:

> A whole race going hedonistic, deciding on pleasure ...
>
> The gay [i.e. pleasure-loving] elements of society had divided into two main streams, one flowing towards Palm Beach and Deauville, and the other, much smaller, towards the summer Riviera. One could get away with more on the summer Riviera, and whatever happened seemed to have something to do with art. From 1926 to 1929, the great years of the Cap d'Antibes, this corner of France was dominated by a group quite distinct from that American society which is dominated by Europeans. Pretty much of anything went at Antibes – by 1929, at the most gorgeous paradise for swimmers on the Mediterranean no one swam any more, save for a short hang-over dip at noon.[1]

Fitzgerald further discriminates between the pleasure-seeking, outgoing life-style of the first half of the 1920s and the darker mood of the end of the period:

> By this time [1927] contemporaries of mine had begun to disappear into the dark maw of violence. A classmate killed his wife and himself on Long Island, another tumbled 'accidently' from a skyscraper in Philadelphia, another purposely from a skyscraper in New York. One was killed in a speak-easy in Chicago; another was beaten to death in a speak-easy in New York and crawled home to the Princeton Club to die; still another had his skull crushed by a maniac's axe in an insane asylum where he was confined. These are not catastrophes that I went out of my

way to look for – these were my friends; moreover, these things happened not during the depression but during the boom.[2]

He concludes:

> It ended two years ago [1929], because the utter confidence which was its essential prop received an enormous jolt, and it didn't take long for the flimsy structure to settle earthward. And after two years the Jazz Age seems as far away as the days before the War. *It was borrowed time anyhow* [italics mine] ...[3]

He is speaking of Americans, or, more precisely, of 'the whole upper tenth of a nation', but the phrase 'It was borrowed time anyhow' could well apply to Dick Diver. By the end of the novel, as Dick wordlessly encourages Nicole to break the bonds that tie them together, he knows he has been living on 'borrowed time' for the last ten years, through the 1920s.

In another of the essays, 'Early Success' (1937), Fitzgerald looks back on the years when he was a struggling young writer and on the excitement of the moment in 1919 when his first novel, *This Side of Paradise*, was accepted by a publisher, so that the young man with cardboard in his shoes could pay off his small debts: he 'woke up every morning with a world of ineffable toploftiness and promise'.[4] He equates his own elation and success with the earlier boom years of post-war America: 'America was going on the greatest, gaudiest spree in history and there was going to be plenty to tell about it. The whole golden boom was in the air ...'[5] Fitzgerald suggests that for the young man of twenty, early success creates the delusion of his own grand destiny. By contrast, a man who achieves success at thirty knows that his own effort is important, while the man of forty who has known what it is to struggle for years values his own contribution most of all. These are generalizations which readers do not have to endorse, but they represent Fitzgerald's thinking about his own career and life at the time he was working on the novel, and are of interest in relation to Dick Diver.

Young Dr Richard Diver

The young Dr Richard Diver who is formally introduced at the beginning of the flashback section in Book II (pp. 129–32) is already valuable in 1917, 'too much of a capital investment' (p. 129) to be sent to the trenches. By this time he is enjoying his 'heroic period' (p. 130), he is 'Lucky Dick' who has a bright career ahead of him. Yet Dick has some passing doubts about his own capabilities: his body is fit, he is a perfect physical specimen of an American upbringing, but he wonders about the calibre of his mind and his capacity to compete with Europeans. He feels that life has been too easy for him and that he has not matured through experience. He laughs at his own capacity to find rather romantic phrases for hard experience, but he has no knowledge of the reality by which to develop judgement. The 'price of his intactness was incompleteness' (p. 131). There is something rather paradoxical about the balancing of those two words: 'intactness' carries an obvious overtone of virginity – not that Dick is sexually inexperienced, as the discreet reference to 'two nice girl visitors' in Vienna implies (p. 130) – but he is emotionally untested and untried, and this is the source of his 'incompleteness'. Dick's personality has not matured – the implication being that this is essentially an American weakness. The narrating voice intrudes upon this introduction of the young Dr Richard Diver to emphasize his lack of judgement: he holds too many illusions about life and is ill equipped to deal with a serious situation involving his emotions or requiring mature decisions:

> Dick got up to Zurich on less Achilles' heels than would be required to equip a centipede, but with plenty – the illusions of eternal strength and health, and of the essential goodness of people; illusions of a nation, the lies of generations of frontier mothers who had to croon falsely, that there were no wolves outside the cabin door [p. 132].

Dick's naïveté is a characteristic of the American male, the result of American history. The men who opened up the vast American continent could not have achieved such a conquest if for one moment they had acknowledged to themselves how terrifying that unknown territory ahead of them was. Dick's American identity is an important factor in his story.

As a climax to the opening chapter of Book II the narrator addresses himself directly to the reader, to the effect that the testing of Dick Diver's emotional maturity is about to begin in Zurich in 1919, with his return to Dr Dohmler's clinic and his resumed acquaintance with the young American patient Nicole Warren. Dick is likened to an American hero, General Ulysses S. Grant, who is unaware that 'an intricate destiny' (p. 132) as a soldier in the American Civil War and later as President awaits him. There is, however, irony in the paralleling of these two American 'destinies', since – and this is one reason why the structure of the novel is important – having read Book I and encountered the older Dick wasting his life in trivialities, the reader already knows what the younger Dick's 'destiny' is: it is to be the guardian of the pleasure or 'fun' of a wealthy set. The tone of the closing sentence is mocking: 'Best to be reassuring – Dick Diver's moment now began' (p. 132). Yet the sentence before this expresses the sadness anyone may feel when matching two mental images: that of the man one knows in his middle age as 'rounded', having put on weight and learned to compromise, and that of the young dreamer he once was who expected so much of life: 'Moreover it is confusing to come across a youthful photograph of some one known in a rounded maturity and gaze with a shock upon a fiery, wiry, eagle-eyed stranger' (p. 132).

To return to Fitzgerald's autobiographical writing, the essay 'Early Success' comments on the existence of these two selves in his own life. He speaks of a moment during his stay on the Riviera when he was driving along the coast road in the evening 'with the whole French Riviera twinkling on the sea below'[6] and experienced a moment of intense emotion: 'It was not Monte Carlo I was looking at. It was back into the mind of the young man with cardboard soles who had walked the streets of New York. I was him again – for an instant I had the good fortune to share his dreams, I who had no more dreams of my own.' It was a moment never to be recaptured: 'But never again as during that all too short period when he and I were one person, when the fulfilled future and the wistful past were mingled in a single gorgeous moment – when life was literally a dream.'[7] Book I of *Tender is the Night* presents the sadly fulfilled future in all its seeming glamour, but Book II returns briefly to the wistful past with all its dreams. Such dreams, which constitute the essential quality of youth, may be delusive, but they are necessary, since without them one can never experience the moment of ecstasy expressed in Keats's 'Ode to a Nightingale'. Fitzgerald recaptures intensity of feeling for one such brief, ecstatic moment on that Riviera road in the evening, when his real self and the romantic young man he once was seem to come together. The older Dick Diver never does so. His tragedy is that he knows the loss of this vital spark of imagination, spontaneous hope and feeling is his own responsibility.

In the title essay, 'The Crack-Up' (1936), Fitzgerald develops some of his ideas on this fusion of youthful inexperience and mature experience. The title refers to his own mental breakdown, when he suddenly realized that 'ten years this side of forty-nine . . . I had prematurely cracked',[8] and the essay is an analysis of its progress. He defines it as the kind that comes from within: 'There is another sort of blow that comes from within – that you don't feel until it's too late to do anything about it, until you realize with finality that in some regard you will never be as good a man again.'[9] It is worth quoting in full Fitzgerald's comments upon the need in life to be able to discern reality and to shape it to one's ideals.

Before I go on with this short history, let me make a general observation – the test of a first-rate intelligence is the ability to hold two opposed ideas in the mind at the same time, and still retain the ability to function. One should, for example, be able to see that things are hopeless and yet be determined to make them otherwise. This philosophy fitted on to my early adult life, when I saw the improbable, the implausible, often the 'impossible', come true. Life was something you dominated if you were any good. Life yielded easily to intelligence and effort, or to what proportion could be mustered of both.[9]

Fitzgerald records in this essay the draining away of his confidence in his ability to shape his own life. In his twenties he believed he could hold the balance between dream and reality, between the inevitability of failure and the determination to succeed, between 'the dead hand of the past and the high intentions of the future'.[8] Now, near the end of his thirties,

I began to realize that for two years my life had been a drawing on resources that I did not possess, but I had been mortgaging myself physically and spiritually up to the hilt. What was the small gift of life given back in comparison to that? – when there had once been a pride of direction and a confidence in enduring independence.[10]

His mental breakdown meant 'being an unwilling witness of an execution, the disintegration of one's own personality'.[11] There had been a 'leak through which, unknown to myself, my enthusiasm and my vitality had been steadily and prematurely trickling away',[12] so that now he found himself in the position of having no sense of himself and no self-respect: 'So there was not an "I" any more.'[13] In this essay Fitzgerald claims that 'One harassed and despairing night'[12] he went off alone, drove a thousand miles, booked a cheap hotel room in some drab little town where no one knew him, and there thought his position over. He resolved that he would be less concerned for others, less ethically aspiring; he would drop his old idealism, since he could no longer fulfil the obligations that life had set for him, or that he had set for himself: 'why not slay the empty shell who had been posturing at it for four years? . . . There was to be no more giving of myself.'[14] He concludes it is impossible for an adult to retain his youthful ambition to be finer than he is, some kind of superhuman figure, since this only brings unhappiness in the end – 'that end that comes to our youth and hope'.[15] Finally, he parallels his own depression with the economic Depression that began in 1929, hitting America so hard during the next decade: 'my recent experience parallels the wave of despair that swept the nation when the Boom was over.'[16] For there is a price to pay: the man who rejects his idealism as an impossible youthful dream has to reject part of himself, some of his deepest values, including his sense that truth is possible in life.

The mature Dick Diver

It would be a mistake to identify Fitzgerald's fictional character, Dick Diver, totally with his creator. For one thing, in writing about himself in these essays, Fitzgerald is in a way fictionalizing himself. Yet the autobiographical elements in Dick Diver's personality and situation are clear enough to offer a pointer to Fitzgerald's thinking about the central character in the novel he took so long to write. His essays spell out some of the features of Dick's personality which are presented obliquely in *Tender is the Night*, particularly towards the end, when Dick's loss of the sense of his own identity has to be interpreted through the clues that Nicole's perceptions give. Fitzgerald's account of his own drive on that 'harassed and despairing night' to the drab little town where no one knew him echoes Dick's withdrawal from the Riviera and subsequent career in smaller and smaller towns in America described in the final two paragraphs (pp. 337–8). Dick Diver, it seems, is permanently seeking, in this series of obscure little towns, to regain a sense of himself as he had been ten years previously. The pile of papers on his desk testifies to that. From her secure position in France, Nicole likes to think of him biding his time, once again like the national hero General Grant before the Civil War called him to a destiny of glory and eminence. The novel itself offers no such hope. Dick Diver is deliberately rendered a distant figure whose identity is signified by no more than a postmark on an envelope. The reader cannot identify with him in any way. The final words of the novel cut off all hope for Dick: he is 'almost certainly ... in one town or another', an exile in his own country who is always seeking, and never finding, the role and fulfilment that his brilliant prospects, rapidly sketched at the beginning of Book II, had seemed to offer.

The point has already been made that the structure with its three different viewpoints is an important device for presenting Dick's story. The gaze of the two women, Rosemary and Nicole, is concentrated on Dick: *his* gaze turns increasingly inwards as he recognizes his failure and its causes, until he feels he has no centre of self, no identity of his own, left. Dick Diver is the focus of narrative interest. For the greater part of the novel his are the judgements with which the reader identifies, yet the shifts of viewpoint and the persistent presence of the narrating voice distance the reader from Dick and enforce judgement on his failure.

Significant points relating to Dick Diver

The world of Dick's creation

(*i*) BOOK I, pp. 14–30 and 34–7

Rosemary's eyes on the beach create the reader's first impressions of Dick Diver. He is 'the man in the jockey cap' (p. 14); he is the centre of attention, not only of his own exclusive little group, but of all the others on the beach, who strain to catch what he is saying (p. 15); he creates laughter (p. 15); he generates excitement (p. 19); his voice seems to woo people (p. 28) with promises of opening up 'whole new worlds ... of magnificent possibilities' (p. 25); his bright blue eyes invite people into his world and attract their liking and trust (p. 20); he flatters people who talk to him with his total attention (p. 28); he behaves with tact and courtesy (p. 25); he is the object of love and respect from his little group (p. 26); he brings to the ordinary day on the beach a touch of style and distinction as he organizes his friends' enjoyment like a gourmet of pleasure (p. 30); he makes Rosemary feel that in drawing her into his world he will take care of her (p. 30).

Nicole's critical intelligence as she walks in her garden counters this series of impressions, for she penetrates beneath surface appearances. Dick's intense exhilaration, which sweeps everyone along, is followed by moods of intense depression (p. 36); he manages to conceal this from all but herself; he enjoys being admired or adored by people and arousing their uncritical love, but when he stops to think about this he is aware of the sheer waste and trivialization of his own personality (p. 36); he has an intuitive understanding of people, by his tact and sympathy gaining their trust so that they are eager to share the happiness and excitement that his amusing world seems to offer (p. 37).

The reader has already observed Rosemary's uncritical response and her eager hero-worship of him. Nicole, through her six years' knowledge of Dick, is aware of what follows. By 1925 Dick can only tolerate people who totally accept the world of his fabrication: as soon as they begin to question it, 'at the first flicker of doubt as to its all-inclusiveness', he withdraws, he evaporates before their eyes (p. 37).

Dick needs other people's total belief in order to sustain his own faith that this world of 'fun' he constructs is the world that he wants.

(*ii*) BOOK II, pp. 187–8

Dick's growing inability to accept the world he has so carefully constructed for six years is an important element of the scenes in 1925. The reader is made aware of the moral and emotional strain with which he lives. At the point in Book II where the narrative returns to the Riviera in 1925 after the flashback sequence, Dick's consciousness becomes the focus of interest. He feels trapped. Almost everything in his life has been bought with Nicole's money – their private little fantasy of a villa on the Riviera, their luxurious life-style and possessions – and although he has tried to maintain a personal independence, this is really only a token gesture (p. 187). Moreover the economic boom has increased Nicole's wealth to such an extent that his attempts to work seem ridiculous, while her emotional and mental needs dominate whatever he tries to do (p. 188). Immobilized by her desire to own him, he feels it increasingly difficult to maintain the pretence of being happy in a life confined to home, where he feels himself watched all the time. The fact that he cannot even play the tune he wants to ('Tea for Two') for fear of giving pain to Nicole by reminding her of Rosemary brings home to Dick what a life of pretence he has been leading (p. 188); his existence now seems empty.

The cracks in Dick's carefully constructed world of charm and style are beginning to appear. As he confesses to Rosemary four years later, 'The change came a long way back – but at first it didn't show. The manner remains intact for some time after the morale cracks' (Book III, p. 307).

Dick's crack-up

(*i*) BOOK I, p. 103

The passage where Dick stands in the dingy Paris street, uncertain what to do about his feelings for Rosemary and troubled by some deeper moral problem, has been examined in Chapter 2 (p. 42).

(*ii*) BOOK II, p. 206–12

Nicole's breakdown in the Swiss fairground brings his own suppressed violence and tension to the surface. This is analysed in Chapter 5 (pp. 85, 92, 95).

(*iii*) BOOK II, pp. 219–23

Dick has been forced to seek relief from the tension of his life with Nicole by taking a walking holiday alone in Austria 'for his soul's sake' (p. 220). This is the first time in their married life they have been separated, but it marks the beginning of a series of separations. In Innsbruck one evening

Dick begins to probe his problems (p. 220): 'He had lost himself ... he had been swallowed up like a gigolo'; once 'he had cut through things, solving the most complicated equations as the simplest problems', now he cannot; he recognizes that he had begun to want money as a reaction against his boyhood experience of watching his clergyman father struggle to make ends meet. This is an important insight on Dick's part regarding his relationship to the world of wealth.

At this point Dick still feels he possesses the resolution – or willpower – to overcome his problems: he will not go on wasting his time and energies trying to teach his values to the wealthy. The images Fitzgerald uses to convey Dick's sense of his own strength are masculine and aggressive ones – images of war: his 'spear had been blunted'; 'his arsenal [had been] locked up in the Warren safety-deposit vaults' (p. 220).

Yet it is significant that before he embarks on this introspection Dick has been thinking of Nicole in one of her most appealing and attractive moods. Immediately afterwards, as he walks alone in the darkness of the hotel garden, he is captivated by a woman's form: she is merely a shadow, a 'black frieze' on the foliage of the bushes (p. 221), but he is momentarily tempted and entranced, troubled by an impulse of desire after years of being faithful to Nicole. To Dick, women at their most mysterious are always desirable and a temptation: he is sexually aroused when his romantic imagination is stimulated, just as Nicole, a beautiful shell of a young girl, aroused his tenderness when he first saw her (Book I, p. 134).

(*iv*) BOOK II, pp. 189–97

The self-awareness that Dick attains here by confronting his own person-ality has already been vividly presented to the reader on a previous occasion, two years earlier in 1925, during the skiing holiday in Gstaad. When Franz urges him to become his partner in a clinic that has just appeared on the market, Dick, distracted from bringing his intellect to bear upon the question by the 'yellow glint in Baby's eyes' (p. 192) and also by the presence in the room of a girl on holiday whose movements and nearness he senses rather than notices (pp. 192–4) (he 'formed imaginary pictures of the prospect as a preliminary to any exercise of judgment' (p. 193)), is angered when Baby, who is looking out for investments for the increased Warren wealth resulting from the boom, comes out with her typically insensitive remark that 'we' must think Franz's offer over (p. 194), but bottles up his rage inside himself, realizing that these powerful women will never understand that a man's pride is his vulnerable spot (p. 195). Dick's attractiveness and good manners have become a form of self-protection behind which he can retreat and conceal all the affronts to his pride that the Warren wealth makes, and he expresses his frustrated anger and injured pride only obliquely when he says, 'There's too much good manners' (p. 195). He is speaking of himself, but nobody understands this; he goes on: 'but if you spend your life sparing people's feelings and feeding their vanity, you get so you can't distinguish what *should* be respected in them' (p. 196). He knows that he is compromising himself by pandering to the vanity of the rich, and when the young Englishman who has been swept along in the tow of Baby's wealth says coldly that Dick isn't trying to understand him, Dick thinks to himself: 'This is what I'll get if I begin saying what I think' (p. 196). When he does say what he thinks of Baby, it is to the lift doors which have slashed shut behind Nicole (p. 197). Two days later the matter is settled as the women want it. As Fitzgerald uses those images of male aggression which have already been commented on, he implies that it is Dick's sense of his manhood which suffers. It is some deep feeling of himself as a man of honour and integrity that is being violated.

(v) BOOK II, pp. 222–3

When the news of his father's death reaches him on his solitary holiday in Innsbruck, Dick is again forced to reflect upon his life. Although his father has always been the major influencing force in his system of values, Dick recognizes the gulf between their lives. Whereas he has not lived up to his intentions (p. 223), his father, despite growing up in 'the gilded age' (p. 223), the period of industrial American expansion when fortunes like that of the Warrens were made, had always maintained a picture of the world in which the values of a Virginian gentleman were sufficient still to see him through life, happy to stand by his older American code of ' "good instincts," honor, courtesy, and courage' (p. 233). This is essentially a male code of honour, and it is the ideal of manhood that Dick feels he has betrayed by becoming 'a gigolo' (p. 220), purchased by the Warren wealth.

(vi) BOOK II, pp. 239–56

Dick's drunken bout in Rome marks the first of a series of humiliations he brings upon himself. Having realized at the end of his affair with Rosemary that he no longer seems 'to bring people happiness any more' (p. 239), he drops all attempts to keep up pretences. He is drinking heavily, savagely imposing his own mood of pent-up anger and despair upon his surroundings. His dance with the young English girl in the bar has none of the aura of mystery and charm that previously characterized his meetings with women (p. 243). Not surprisingly, she slips away. He knocks over a cigar stand in his drunken unsteadiness (p. 244); it is he who initiates violence by hitting the grinning policeman 'a smashing left beside the jaw' (p. 246). Fitzgerald emphasizes the brutality of the encounter by using language of clubbing, smashing, splintering and stamping. The effect of this experience on Dick is profound. He has been made to feel criminal, and he knows that he will never lose his sense of humiliation and self-loathing, that he can never be quite his old self again (p. 254). Dick's sense of alienation from himself is rendered even more effective in the narrative by the fact that the waiting crowd mistakes him for a child rapist and murderer and reviles him too (p. 255). Dick is almost willing to believe he is the man they hate; he feels guilty because he has betrayed his best instincts and aspirations. This is discussed further on pp. 86, 99.

This episode leads to the break-up of Dick's life. It gives Kaethe Gregorovious the chance to tell her husband that Dick is no longer 'a serious man' (p. 261), and puts such pressure on Dick's personality that he punishes himself by overwork (p. 262) and by subsequent self-humiliation on the Riviera. Whereas he had once charmed people, he now deliberately seeks to antagonize them in order to punish himself further. His drinking does not help, as it slows down his mental reactions, giving his critics an advantage over him.

(*vii*) BOOK III, pp. 272–6

Once Mr Morris has removed his son from the clinic on the grounds that Dick is not qualified to help the young man's alcoholism when he himself smells of drink, Dick's honesty forces him to consider the justice of this charge: 'He was averaging a half-pint of alcohol a day, too much for the system to burn up' (p. 274). He resolves to cut his consumption by half for the sake of professional ethics (p. 274). When Franz returns soon after this (p. 275), Dick hesitates 'on the verge of the truth' about the affair. He tells Franz of the encounter with Mr Morris, saying, 'You must know I'm the last man to abuse liquor.' The detail that 'His eyes and Franz's glinted on each other, pair on pair' seems to imply that, while Dick is deliberately minimizing his intake, Franz has other views on the matter. When Franz decides to adopt a stern moral tone, he assumes 'a suitable mask' (p. 276) in order to assert a superior position over Dick. But Dick is sickened by polite posturing, and his innate honesty will not let him keep up pretences: 'To explain, to patch – these were not natural functions at their age – better to continue with the cracked echo of an old truth in the ears' (p. 276). Dick's honesty forces him to acknowledge he has lost interest. His professional concerns have long been 'dissolving into a lifeless mass' (p. 276), they have lost their meaning for him.

Dick's withdrawal

(*i*) BOOK III, pp. 287–96

After their drunken cook Augustine has got the better of Dick to the tune of a hundred francs and left with her dignity intact, Dick and Nicole dine in Nice to get away from the scene of such unpleasantness. Nicole's comment 'I've ruined you' (p. 287) touches Dick to the core.

Although he retains his pleasant demeanour and even tries to be, as of old, a 'conspirator for pleasure, mischief, profit, and delight' (p. 288), his old magic has gone. On the Golding yacht, which he insists they visit, he is publicly humiliated by the unpleasant Lady Caroline Sibly-Biers (p. 293), when his heavy irony is employed too late to be effective. He checks his impulse to use this weapon on Nicole – or even hurt her physically – when he sees her fear of him (p. 294). He merely declines into drunken passivity and allows Nicole to feel her freedom (p. 296).

(*ii*) BOOK III, pp. 299–300

When Nicole makes her first bid for independence by throwing the jar of camphor rub to Tommy Barban (p. 299), Dick remains passive and inert. The narrative focuses on Nicole's consciousness, and so the reader is given no indication of what is going on in Dick's mind as he lies on his bed. The situation is, perhaps, all the more poignant because of this. Nicole looks at 'the stricken man', 'aware of the sin she had committed against him' (p. 300). At this point Fitzgerald introduces a rather strange image: Nicole wonders what Dick will 'feed on while she must still continue her dry suckling at his lean chest' (p. 300). The image emphasizes Dick's role as a giver of sustenance who has drained himself of vitality in the process of nurturing Nicole: but it also, metaphorically, gives him feminine attributes, and thus reinforces the idea that he has lost his manhood through allowing himself to be swept into the life of the idle rich.

(*iii*) BOOK III, pp. 300–310

Fitzgerald delineates Dick's crack-up through trivial and seemingly insignificant events. His further public humiliation on the beach among his former admirers is presented through Nicole's coldly critical observation. What is going on inside him is left to the reader's imagination. Dick's desperate bid to display his male prowess by lifting up a man on his shoulders on the water-ski board (pp. 304–6) fails because he is tired and not the man he once was, and his vanity is stung by his failure to impress Rosemary's entourage of young men. Nicole watches 'the old game of flattery beginning again' with Rosemary (p. 303), but knows Dick has lost his skill; 'his old expertness with people' has deserted him. Rosemary remembers she has recently heard gossip that Baby Warren's sister 'had thrown herself away on a dissipated doctor' (p. 308) who is now 'not received anywhere any more'.

By making Dick the object of other characters' speculation Fitzgerald very effectively portrays his isolation. That a word like 'dissipated' should be going the rounds among the very people to whom Dick has given his energies both disturbs the reader and reveals the extent of Dick's moral collapse. It conveys how easy it is to be rejected by people whose only goal is entertainment.

(*iv*) BOOK III, pp. 323–4

Once Nicole has embarked on her affair with Tommy Barban, her sense of having betrayed all the good times she has shared with Dick makes her want to re-establish contact with him. When she touches him he rejects her, saying, 'I can't do anything for you any more. I'm trying to save myself' (p. 323). It is actually Nicole's battle that is described in its intensity as the two of them sit silently together, having reached a point where no words are possible. Nicole has to force herself to remember all her old resentment of his authority over her, and the new authority that her wealth gives her, in order to cut him out of her emotional life. Dick has no weapon and no will to fight. When Nicole finally walks away, weeping from the effort but satisfied she is in the right, according to her new values, he knows what has happened. All he can do is lean in exhaustion over the parapet: 'The case was finished. Doctor Diver was at liberty' (p. 324). Fitzgerald uses Dick's professional title deliberately here. When in 1932 the final shape of the novel began to emerge, he wrote in his Notebook as a memorandum to himself:

> The novel should do this: show a man who is a natural idealist, a spoiled priest, giving in for various causes to the ideas of the haute bourgeoisie, and in his rise to the top of the social world losing his idealism, his talent and turning to drink and dissipation. Background one in which the leisure class is at the truly most brilliant and glamorous . . .[17]

(*v*) BOOK III, pp. 336–7

Dick's farewell to the beach he has 'created' is his final act of withdrawal. He has taken a big drink of brandy before leaving the villa, and now he feels fine, rather as 'a man should . . . at the end of a good dinner' (p. 336). When he meets Mary Minghetti he is tempted to exert his old charm on her, but cannot keep it up because he can no longer delude himself that pleasing people by his attractiveness is of any interest to him. Mocking laughter rises in him and so he 'switches off' the light of his charm (p. 337).

His final gesture is puzzling. Rising from his seat on the hotel terrace, he 'raised his right hand and with a papal cross he blessed the beach from the high terrace. Faces turned upward from several umbrellas' (p. 337). Dick is slightly drunk. Is this a gesture of mockery against the people whose pleasure he has served and who are now in possession of his creation? Is the mockery directed ironically against himself? Alternatively, is it an act of blessing and compassion for the people who are morally adrift in their unthinking and egotistical pursuit of pleasure? This would make it an expression of moral seriousness and authority. It is possible that there is something of all these impulses in his benediction. Dick is too complex a character to assert an easy superiority over others: his growing bitterness against them has also been directed against himself. Yet in his recent encounter with Mary Minghetti and Lady Caroline Sibly-Biers, when he was instrumental in buying them free of a serious police charge for a moral offence, he sat in the police cell, 'looking at the stone floor, like a priest in the confessional' (p. 326), torn between the desire to laugh ironically at the situation and the wish for an old-fashioned punishment for the total lack of awareness in the two women of their own moral laxity.

If, at the end of the novel, Dick sees other people's moral faults, he does so from the vantage point of having recognized his own and suffered for them. The final gesture, if it is a blessing, may be the act of a mature and compassionate man. What he has recognized about himself is that it is his personality to want to be loved, particularly by women (p. 325), and to need to exert 'the old fatal pleasingness, the old forceful charm' (p. 324). Dick's painful self-knowledge gives him a moral stature in the novel which no other character possesses, even though it also destroys him, turning him into a wanderer, always 'running away from things' (p. 321) and never finding the self he wants to be.

4. Women Characters:
'You Are Attractive to Women, Dick'

In all Fitzgerald's novels the women seem to be survivors by nature. They often possess an essential toughness which the male characters lack. At the end of *Tender is the Night* the women are left in full possession of the beach which Dick has created. They seem to be able to handle the future, while Dick and Abe North remain trapped in a past which has failed to fulfil their expectations. It is interesting that both young women, Rosemary and Nicole, cut 'the umbilical cord' – Rosemary from her mother in Book I and Nicole from Dick, her father-figure, in Book III. The young women assert their independence and enjoy the freedom which the 1920s and the security of their wealth permit them. When she sleeps with Tommy Barban, Nicole 'welcomed the anarchy of her lover' (Book III, p. 320). Once away from Dick's controlling influence, which he exercises effortlessly in Book I, the women possess few scruples and no inhibitions. By contrast, Dick, having broken free of the essentially male moral values of his ancestors, who helped to found America, is driven to despair by a sense of his betrayal of fundamental 'decencies' which give meaning to life. The only female character who is not a born survivor is the unnamed woman patient in the clinic whose illness seems to have deprived her of her femininity and sexuality (Book II, pp. 201–4, and Book III, pp. 262–3).

The unnamed woman patient

On her admittance she had been exceptionally pretty – now she was a living agonizing sore. All blood tests had failed to give a positive reaction and the trouble was unsatisfactorily catalogued as nervous eczema. For two months she had lain under it, as imprisoned in the Iron Maiden [Book II, p. 202].

She says she is sharing the fate of all women of her time who have tried to compete with men. Dick looks on her as an artist who has tried to force her consciousness into new areas of experience and who has not been strong enough to bear the strain. While Franz diagnoses her as a victim of syphilis (p. 262), Dick sees in her a sensitive, suffering victim, whether of her own follies or of others'. He clearly identifies with her emotionally, and through the way he positions the woman's death at that particular point in Dick's deterioration, Fitzgerald also intends an identification of the two.

American women

Apart from this one unnamed woman artist, Fitzgerald is critical of American women in the novel. The authorial voice offers a number of hostile judgements about the influence of American women in preventing their men from attaining intellectual maturity, even to the extent of infantilizing them. For instance, at the beginning of the flashback section of Book II, Dick is introduced as a young man waiting to be called to 'an intricate destiny', but his weaknesses are referred to as a source of potential danger: 'the illusions of eternal strength and health, and of the essential goodness of people; illusions of a nation, the lies of generations of frontier mothers who had to croon falsely, that there were no wolves outside the cabin door' (p. 132). Later in Book II, when Baby Warren has aroused the American Consul and bullied him into action to obtain Dick's release, the authorial voice comments: 'the American Woman, aroused, stood over him; the clean-sweeping irrational temper that had broken the moral back of a race and made a nursery out of a continent, was too much for him. He rang for the vice-consul – Baby had won' (p. 253). The ironic implication of the capital letter deprives 'the American Woman' of moral seriousness and converts her into a stern nanny who over-protects her charges.

Baby Warren

Baby Warren seems to enjoy her childhood name, a name which emphasizes her American identity. Apart from Lady Caroline Sibly-Biers, she is the only woman in the novel who does not succumb to Dick's particular form of charm. He does not possess any of the attributes which hold attraction for her: he is not English, nor an aristocrat, nor is he wealthy. Dick maintains an ironic attitude towards her, and as she is presented largely through his observation of her, the reader judges her through his eyes. Fitzgerald handles her almost as a crude caricature, but he appears to imply that she is turning herself into one, since her wealth determines her life and her values.

Dick first encounters her in her role of Nicole's guardian, a position she obviously does not relish. At no point does she express any interest in the cause of her young sister's illness, or tenderness for her. She likes to find someone to blame 'for the catastrophe in her sister's life' (Book II, p. 233), and Dick wonders just how much knowledge or suspicion she represses (pp. 234–5).

At their first meeting her personality is sketched through her relationship with men:

> But Baby Warren wanted to talk to Dick, wanted to talk to him with the impetus that sent her out vagrantly toward all new men, as though she were on an inelastic tether and considered that she might as well get to the end of it as soon as possible. She crossed and recrossed her knees frequently in the manner of tall restless virgins [Book II, p. 167].

The image of an 'inelastic tether' conveys the tension within a woman who is afraid of sex and yet enjoys the power her wealth gives her over men. Her relationships with them seem to be arid, without tenderness. At the end of the novel, ten years older, Baby is still 'considering whether or not to marry the latest candidate for her hand and money, an authenticated Hapsburg' (Book III, p. 335). As she 'dries out', by which Fitzgerald means that she is becoming more spinsterish, her romantic affairs increasingly have more interest for her as a source of conversation than of emotional interest, just as her engagement to the young English aristocrat killed in the war has had all these years: 'Her emotions had their truest existence in the telling of them' (p. 335). Like those candidates for her wealth and hand, Dick's value consists in his usefulness. *They* provide her with something to talk about; Dick contributes the medical expertise she needs for her sister.

As soon as they meet Baby gets down to business, fast and without tact. Her wealth gives her the right to disregard other people's feelings. Dick recognizes her total lack of imagination, and he sees 'something wooden and onanistic[1] about her' (Book II, p. 168). Although he remains polite, internally he engages in the only response possible in such a grotesque situation – mocking laughter: 'A burst of hilarity surged up in Dick, the Warrens were going to buy Nicole a doctor – You got a nice doctor you can let us use?' (p. 169). Dick wrongly assumes that she wants him to marry Nicole so that he can look after her fully. The narrating voice corrects him: 'Doctor Diver was not the sort of medical man she could envisage in the family' (p. 174). He is not good enough: 'She only wanted to use him innocently as a convenience.'

Six years later, during the skiing holiday in Gstaad, Dick is less ready to laugh at 'her cold rich insolence' (Book II, p. 195) when, in reply to Franz's proposal that they go into partnership in a clinic, she comments, 'We must think it over carefully' (p. 194). She has a nose for a good investment, and as she seems to control her sister's finances, her voice matters. By now, Dick is particularly sensitive to the ruin of his ambitions, and his understanding of the real meaning of her words is bitter: ' "We must think it over carefully –" ' and the unsaid lines back of that: "We own you, and you'll admit it sooner or later. It is absurd to keep up the pretence of independence" ' (p. 195). Later that evening he begins to make a savage comment on Baby to Nicole, but finishes it rather tamely in his thoughts: 'Baby is a trivial, selfish woman' (p. 197).

On his disastrous trip to Rome some years later, Dick meets Baby again and tries to draw her out about her inner life, but it is obvious that she has none. Her voice takes on a tinny note, as though she were playing an old guitar solo yet again (Book II, p. 236). He finds himself admiring her consistency and single-mindedness, and manages to maintain a facetious relationship with her, although her snobbishness remains nearly intolerable to him.

Baby Warren is a product of the Warren wealth. Her presence in the novel stresses the power of wealth, and she is introduced at key points in Dick's life when her money counts. In Rome she is perfectly ready to discard Dick if Nicole no longer needs him: ' "You think she'd be happier with somebody else?" Baby thought aloud suddenly. "Of course it could be arranged" ' (Book II, p. 235). Fitzgerald handles her attempts to obtain Dick's release from prison as grotesque comedy. She acts like an avenging angel, ruthlessly using the family name, but it is the possible scandal that motivates her rather than concern for Dick. Her triumph is made the climax of Book II: 'It had been a hard night but she had the satisfaction of feeling that, whatever Dick's previous record was, they now possessed a moral superiority over him for as long as he proved of any use' (p. 256). In the final beach scene, when Nicole seems in danger of being sentimental about all that Dick has done for her, Baby dismisses him: 'That's what he was educated for' (Book III, p. 335). Fitzgerald makes her a crude representative of the American wealth and power without responsibility that destroys Dick.

Mrs Elsie Speers

A rather more enigmatic American woman in the novel is Mrs Speers, Rosemary's mother. Her role is a minor one, but there seems to be a certain ambivalence in it. To begin with, she is presented in terms of approval by the author. Mother and daughter are looking for someone to provide amusement for them as a right they have earned by their hard work. There is no further explanation of their presence until after

Rosemary tells her mother that she has fallen in love with Dick (Book I, p. 20), when the relationship between the two, mother and daughter, is analysed and biographical details are filled in (p. 21), the tone and language both expressing approval. Mrs Speers has moulded her daughter by being herself a model of hard work and loving care, and she has inculcated in her 'a mature distrust of the trivial, the facile and the vulgar' (p. 21). Now that her daughter is an international star she encourages her to be independent and to seek adult experience. She makes a good impression on the Divers at their dinner-party, and Rosemary, watching her, reads approval of Dick in her face which she interprets as ' "the real thing"; it meant permission to go as far as she could' (Book I, p. 40). This is expanded some pages later as a wish that Rosemary should gain experience of love with a suitable man. The widow who forced a film producer to give her sixteen-year-old daughter a chance now wants her to experiment with affairs of the heart: 'Wound yourself or him – whatever happens it can't spoil you because economically you're a boy, not a girl' (Book I, p. 50). In the cause of experience she encourages Rosemary to go and watch the duel between Tommy Barban and McKisco, and Rosemary obeys 'the sure, clear voice that had sent her into the stage entrance of the Odéon in Paris when she was twelve and greeted her when she came out again' (Book I, p. 58).

Rosemary separates from her mother for the first time in her adult life when she goes to Paris with the Divers to be near Dick, and so Mrs Speers fades from her daughter's life except as the recipient of her letters. She reappears briefly in Book II when, after the flashback sequence, the narrative picks up the thread of events in 1925, with the Divers' return to the Riviera for Nicole's recuperation after her breakdown in the Paris hotel. Dick meets Mrs Speers in Cannes, and naturally she is well aware of what has been happening. She tells him that he is the first man Rosemary has ever cared for and that she had given the affair her blessing:

> He saw that no provision had been made for him, or for Nicole, in Mrs Speers' plans – and he saw that her amorality sprang from the conditions of her own withdrawal. It was her right, the pension on which her own emotions had retired. Women are necessarily capable of almost anything in their struggle for survival and can scarcely be convicted of such man-made crimes as 'cruelty.' So long as the shuffle of love and pain went on within proper walls Mrs Speers could view it with as much detachment and humor as a eunuch. She had not even allowed for the possibility of Rosemary's being damaged – or was she certain that she couldn't be? [Book II, p. 180]

Dick is feeling bitter here. He realizes that Mrs Speers has become a spectator of life. As a widow, she has devoted herself so totally to her daughter's life and career that she has no existence of her own and no emotional life either. The word 'eunuch' has an ugly sound in this context. Nonetheless, there seems to be some criticism of the 'amorality' which women develop when they have to survive in a man's world without men of their own. It is difficult to decide whether these are Dick's ideas or the author's own. Mrs Speers seems to have absolved herself from any guilt in letting her daughter play with a man's emotions, provided that the proprieties are observed. Dick's final thought that probably she knows her daughter cannot be emotionally hurt makes mother and daughter seem tough indeed. At this point it is worth looking back at the opening description of the two as they arrive at Gausse's Hotel: 'They wanted high excitement, not from the necessity of stimulating jaded nerves but with the avidity of prize-winning schoolchildren who deserved their vacations' (Book I, p. 12). The word 'avidity' associates them with *greed*: they are greedy for emotional excitement because they think they have earned it. It does not matter if someone else – in this case both Dick and Nicole – gets hurt. This is another example of the discriminations that the novel makes between the moral values of men and the lack of them in women.

Mary North

Mary North is another survivor. Initially, as observed by Rosemary on the beach or at the Villa Diana, she is noticed primarily as an attractive tanned woman with a mischievous smile who takes little part in any conversation: 'Then Mary North with a face so merry that it was impossible not to smile back into the white mirrors of her teeth – the whole area around her parted lips was a lovely little circle of delight' (Book I, p. 43). In Paris she seems merely to exist as the worried appendage of Abe, anxious about his drinking and irresponsibility, but too tactful and self-effacing to remonstrate or make a scene. She is characterized in Book I largely by what other characters notice of her – her white teeth framed by a smiling, tanned face. The only time she breaks out of her repose is when she exclaims in shock at Dick's comment that he may abandon his scientific work.

However, at one point in the Paris scenes the authorial voice does focus on Mary, giving her an importance which she has not had before. It is difficult to know what to make of the final unfinished sentence, though its significance is apparent in Book III after Mary's reintroduction into the narrative. The explanation may be that Fitzgerald felt the need for a link to explain Mary's meteoric – and surely unlikely? – rise to social eminence by her second marriage.

'Good night, dear Dick.' Mary smiled as if she were going to be perfectly happy sitting there on the almost deserted boat. She was a brave, hopeful woman and she was following her husband somewhere, changing herself to this kind of person or that, without being able to lead him a step out of his path, and sometimes realizing with discouragement how deep in him the guarded secret of her direction lay. And yet an air of luck clung about her, as if she were a sort of token ... [Book I, p. 73]

Mary re-enters the narrative in Book III after Dick has severed his connection with the clinic. Fitzgerald offers no explanation of her life in the mean time: 'The journey that had begun in a room over the shop of a paper-hanger in Newark had ended in an extraordinary marriage' (Book III, p. 279). The splendour of her new establishment far outshines the entourage of the Divers, and Dick comments rather maliciously that 'Little Mary North knows what she wants' (p. 279). During their cata-strophic visit to Mary and her second husband, Dick disgraces himself by drinking too much and using words like 'spic' in front of his host, and confesses, 'I'm not much like myself any more' (p. 280). But he causes most offence over the very prosaic matter of the alleged dirty bathwater, when Lanier claims that he has had to bathe in the same water as the child with the skin infection (p. 281). Mary is a determined social climber who will tolerate no behaviour that seems to reflect upon her social position: 'the old unity was split – between them lay the restless social fields that Mary was about to conquer' (p. 282). She is no longer the quiet onlooker, and proves a brusque antagonist in her angry exchange with Dick. The function of this visit is to show how far Dick has deteriorated since the old days of harmony and friendship between the Divers and the Norths. It presents the reader for the first time with evidence of Dick's biting tongue, which he uses without consideration for others' feelings. When Mary complains that he has not listened to her explanations about the customs of her new family, he retorts, 'But you've gotten so damned dull, Mary. I listened as long as I could' (p. 285). Not only is his old charm gone, but he is insensitive to other people.

In the final Riviera scenes Mary is certainly neither accommodating nor self-effacing. Now that she possesses a title she is determined to assert herself socially. She can command a little court of admirers, just as Rosemary can. Nicole judges that Dick is no longer at ease on the beach that was his creation, but is behaving 'like a deposed ruler secretly visiting an old court' (Book III, p. 301). While Rosemary is to be traced by 'the school of little fish who followed her, taking their dazzle from her' (p. 302), Dick points out 'our old friend, Mrs Abrams, playing duchess to Mary North's queen' (p. 307). Mary can now afford to let her glance flicker over her old friends with a look that lets them know they are being cut, although she cannot afford to snub Rosemary, who is with them.

Mary is not only associated with snobbishness and blatant social climbing in these final scenes, but her behaviour with her friend Lady Caroline Sibly-Biers suggests sexual perversion. The two titled ladies find their pleasure in transvestite activities in the poorer part of the city. Dressed as French sailors they pick up two girls, and are enraged when the girls create a scene. Mary panics, fearful of the consequences if her husband should get to hear of her arrest. Her deterioration from the 'brave hopeful woman' of Book I seems complete. Gausse, the hotelier, who is called on with Dick to get them bail, buys off the police and comments, '... women like these women I have never seen before' (Book III, p. 329).

Dick's final conversation on the beach is with Mary. Each of them is eager momentarily to re-establish something of the old relationship – simply because they each need reassurance that they are likeable people and are prepared to use one another for this. When Dick asks for her assurance that she had once liked him, Mary replies: '*Liked* you – I *loved* you. Everybody loved you. You could've had anybody you wanted for the asking' (Book III, p. 337). Presumably she means that in 1925 she would gladly have had an affair with him. It was Dick who set the moral standards in those days, and he had remained faithful to Nicole until Rosemary came along.

In this final meeting Dick is exercising his old charm quite deliberately in order to manipulate Mary and bolster his own ego. He cannot keep it up for long as he knows it is meaningless. Mary's presence on the beach is important in further sharpening the contrasts with the beach scenes in Book I. Her emotions are facile and her friendship with Lady Caroline Sibly-Biers is disturbing, yet her presence, with its reminders of an innocent past, intensifies the poignancy of Dick's deterioration and isolation.

One might question whether Mary's reappearance is contrived. Fitzgerald clearly restored the characters who were present in Book I for reasons of contrast. But the Mary North of Book III is so unlike the smiling woman of Book I that one wonders whether consistency of character was sacrificed to the need to end with a callous world of morally unlikeable people who triumph while Dick fails.

Rosemary Hoyt

The young ingénue

Rosemary Hoyt is handled throughout the novel with detachment and a certain measure of irony. Fitzgerald gives her a central position in Book I by making her consciousness the initial location of the action. Scenes are filtered to the reader through her perception of them. It is worth considering what he achieves by this narrative device.

As Rosemary is a new arrival on the beach, she is an outsider whose gaze takes in all the details of those already in possession of it. Her eyes act as a camera, focusing on their everyday little rituals from a distance, picking out all the seemingly unrelated details of 'the dark people and the light' (p. 14), the exclusive tanned habitués of the beach and the intruding, socially insecure newcomers. Fitzgerald also uses a close-up film technique to introduce Rosemary into the narrative in a way that suggests a studio publicity photograph. The language is rather inflated:

> [She] had magic in her pink palms and her cheeks lit to a lovely flame, like the thrilling flush of children after their cold baths in the evening. Her fine high forehead sloped gently up to where her hair, bordering it like an armorial shield, burst into lovelocks and waves and curlicues of ash blonde and gold. Her eyes were bright, big, clear, wet, and shining, the color of her cheeks was real, breaking close to the surface from the strong young pump of her heart. Her body hovered delicately on the last edge of childhood – she was almost eighteen, nearly complete, but the dew was still on her [pp. 11–12].

It is a strange introduction, almost hostile in its vocabulary. Indeed, a dated word like 'lovelocks' can only be hostile. It certainly does not invite the reader to take her seriously. The rather intimate detail that she is 'nearly complete' implies some sexual experimentation that Collis Clay's gossip later confirms, and presumably informs the reader that she is not the innocent she has just played in her first big film role.

Fitzgerald never allows the reader to forget that Rosemary is a film-star, a new phenomenon of the 1920s, and the product of studio publicity. He achieves this by pictorial techniques such as the opening close-up description of mother and daughter. Rosemary is a new kind of girl, the star with a contract. When she visits Brady, the American film producer, in Monte Carlo she is on familiar ground:

> They were meeting for the first time. Brady was quick and strenuous. As he took her hand she saw him look her over from head to foot, a gesture she recognized

and that made her feel at home, but gave her always a faint feeling of superiority to whoever made it. If her person was property she could exercise whatever advantage was inherent in its ownership [Book I, p. 32].

Rosemary knows that her body and her sexuality are a commodity, but they are her property. They are her bargaining power in professional life.

The author denies Rosemary any sympathetic, intuitive feeling for a situation. The authorial voice states quite categorically that she is too naïve to comprehend the desperation underlying the Divers' social gestures and lives. Quite often she seems to be too busy adjusting her facial responses as though she were acting. When her mother suggests that being in love ought to make her happy, Rosemary reacts obediently: 'Rosemary looked up and gave a beautiful little shiver of her face and laughed. Her mother always had a great influence on her' (p. 31). Under the spell of the Villa Diana and the Divers' charm, Rosemary feels that this is 'the centre of the world' (p. 38). Again she comes under critical attack from the author. She is 'as dewy with belief as a child from one of Mrs Burnett's vicious tracts' (p. 43). Frances Hodgson Burnett was the late-nineteenth-century author of such best-sellers as *Little Lord Fauntleroy*. Presumably Fitzgerald has in mind this prettified hero who does rather well out of his innocence. In that case, Rosemary's innocence is self-conscious enough to ensure that she will not get hurt. She feels that she has earned a moment or two alone with Dick after dinner, and he obligingly takes her for a walk in the garden. However, he is aware of her 'too obvious appeal, the struggle with an unrehearsed scene and unfamiliar words' (p. 48). For him at this time she is just a very pretty girl, and he doesn't want any emotional entanglement with her. He speaks very deliberately of 'we', thereby firmly associating himself with Nicole, and soon 'delivers' her back to Nicole. Later that night Rosemary finds a role for herself in the bizarre duel which brings the Riviera scene to an end in Book I. When she comes upon the forlorn figure of Luis Campion outside the hotel, weeping because his homosexual advances have been rejected, her professional training gives her self-control: 'A scene in a rôle she had played last year swept over her irresistibly and advancing she touched him on the shoulder' (p. 50).

In Paris Rosemary's innocence initially helps her sophisticated companions to relax and forget any 'reservations' about each other (p. 63). The intimate whispered conversation which she overhears between Dick and Nicole as they confess their sexual need for each other startles her (p. 64). She has been regarding them as The Divers, as a child might, but this makes her sexually more aware. Rosemary is growing up. She celebrates her eighteenth birthday and tries to seduce Dick, wanting sexual experience. Dick tries to maintain a kindly, fatherly relationship, and yet it is he, not Rosemary, who begins to feel lost and confused. When she clings to him in the taxi, wearing the new perfume that she has purchased under Nicole's guidance, he 'kissed her without enjoying it. He knew that there was passion there, but there was no shadow of it in her eyes or on her mouth' (p. 74). The emphasis of the narrative is on Dick, not Rosemary. When she begs Dick, 'Take me,' she knows that she is playing one of her greatest roles: 'She was calling on things she had read, seen, dreamed through a decade of convent hours' (p. 75). She is an attractive girl, and Dick has to exercise all his self-control in order to remind them both that this might hurt Nicole. She is ingenuous in throwing herself at Dick in her desire for adult sexual experience:

> Oh, please, I don't care even if I had a baby. I could go into Mexico like a girl at the studio. Oh, this is so different from anything I ever thought – I used to hate it when they kissed me seriously . . . Some of them had great big teeth, but you're all different and beautiful. I want you to do it [p. 76].

Dick makes a comforting little speech, and as soon as he has gone she settles down to her nightly ritual of caring for her best feature, her glorious hair. Rosemary enjoys her role, and quickly recognizes the signs that Dick is becoming interested in her.

The significance of the title of Rosemary's first big film is not apparent to the reader at this point. But when, in Book II, the incestuous relationship between Mr Devereux Warren and his adolescent daughter is recounted, the title takes on a new meaning. *Daddy's Girl*, the film that brought Rosemary Hoyt international stardom, is a childish fantasy, an expensive Hollywood product which blinds masses of people to the realities of life and of emotion. For Nicole the experience of being 'daddy's girl' to her self-indulgent father had been a traumatic one: Rosemary's screen heroine is a plucky and adorable girl. Dick, as a psychologist who is aware of the irony, sees in the final 'lovely' shot of the heroine 'a father complex so apparent that [he] winced for all psychologists at the vicious sentimentality' (Book I, p. 80). The narrating voice adopts a childish style to recount the story of the film, thereby implying that its representation of the triumph of innocence is in itself corrupting and embodies 'all the immaturity of the race [that is, of Americans], cutting a new cardboard paper doll to pass before its empty harlot's mind' (p. 80). Although Dick recognizes the distasteful sentimentality of the film, he enjoys touching shoulders with Rosemary in the darkness at the private showing. Her little ploy of arranging a screen test for Dick does not go down well with these wealthy socialites.

The reception to which Dick takes Rosemary immediately afterwards effects a contrast with the false innocence of her film role. Their hostess is 'another tall rich American girl, promenading insouciantly upon the national prosperity' (p. 85). She is engaged in ripping out the interior of one of the old palatial Parisian houses and modernizing it with steel, silver-gilt and glass. The place reminds Rosemary of a film set. Fitzgerald uses the image of 'a human hand picking up jagged broken glass' to convey the tensions in this roomful of thirty people, mostly women, who are all on the make for something – the hostess, in particular, for an invitation to join Dick's exclusive set on the Riviera – as they eye each other and angle for advantage. Prominent among them are 'the three cobra women' (p. 84), who dissect Dick critically as dated and boring, though one of them acknowledges that 'the party in question can be one of the most charming human beings you have ever met' (p. 84). Rosemary overhears this conversation while she is being more or less propositioned by a 'neat, slick girl with a lovely boy's face' (p. 83). There are certainly sexual undertones in this gathering of female birds of prey, undertones linked with the power of wealth, and the party sets the moral tone which predominates in Book III.

In Paris Rosemary succeeds in making Dick fall in love with her. Her youth and her vitality have an effect on him in their shared little intimacies of conversation in taxis and on stairs. What began for him as an interlude becomes an obsession, while for Rosemary it is an enjoyable experiment which leaves her emotionally untouched: ' "I do love you – I can't change that." It was time for Rosemary to cry, so she cried a little in her handkerchief' (p. 85). Rosemary enjoys the best of both worlds. She is grown up, and yet she still has her mother to confide in. It is the Divers who pay the price.

Rosemary and Nicole seem to move closer together when they go shopping. It is as if spending money creates a bond between them even though their attitudes are different.

It was fun spending money in the sunlight of the foreign city, with healthy bodies under them that sent streams of color up to their faces; with arms and hands, legs and ankles that they stretched out confidently, reaching or stepping with the confidence of women lovely to men [p. 110].

The connection between their power to spend money and their sexual attractiveness is made explicit here. Their beauty is enhanced by their wealth, and throughout the novel both women gain reassurance from this.

Rosemary is misled by the surface gaiety of the Divers' lives and all the signs of their wealth and prestige. Her sense of Dick's social standing makes her enjoy her power over this older man, as it is all part of the game she is playing with the adult world: 'counting benefits, counting hopes, telling off Dick, Nicole, her mother, the director she met yesterday, like stops on a string of beads' (Book I, p. 117). While she is 'playing around with chaos', Rosemary is oblivious of the turmoil in Dick's mind when, for the first time in six years, the certainties in his life with Nicole, a life he has so carefully managed to construct, no longer seem secure. To her, Dick is 'fixed and Godlike' (p. 117). When Rosemary opens her hotel-room door to him, Dick knows that she is incapable of understanding him and is playing with her own sexuality. Her body is 'calculated to a millimeter to suggest a bud yet guarantee a flower' (p. 117). This rather enigmatic metaphor implies both the expensiveness of Rosemary's toilet in attaining just the right measure of allure, and also the degree of her expertise in the sexual game. She rather self-consciously experiments with love-making, but she senses that neither of them is being spontaneous: 'Oh, we're such *actors* – you and I' (p. 118).

Their big scene together is interrupted by the arrival of Abe North with his frightened Mr Peterson in tow, which gives Rosemary a chance to make 'an exit that she had learned young, and on which no director had ever tried to improve' (p. 122). When she returns to find the dead man on her bed, both she and Dick realize that her career is at stake. As a piece of public property, she is obliged by her contract 'to continue rigidly and unexceptionally as "Daddy's Girl"' (p. 124). The irony of Fitzgerald's choice of film title is again evident. To be 'daddy's girl' means to maintain a fantasy morality for public consumption: it may also carry overtones of the sugar daddy, the man who enjoys the pleasures of an erotic relationship by placing them on a firm financial basis.

The film-star on location

When they meet four years later in Rome, Dick feels compelled to pursue her, just as she pursued him, the sophisticated older man, at their first encounter. Dick finds her magnetic now, but recognizes that 'Eighteen might look at thirty-four through a rising mist of adolescence; but twenty-two would see thirty-eight with discerning clarity' (Book II, p. 227). Dick is now demanding and urgent in his desire for her, but she has the skill to hold him off. He insists on knowing about her relationships with other

73

men, and it is Rosemary's turn to feel disappointment: he assumes he can take possession of her, just like all the other men.

As a glamorous star of 1928 Rosemary is allowed to display her sex appeal in the new film she is making. Dick really has a secondary place in her life, as she has to handle her leading man, Nicotera, too, and work in the sweaty heat of Rome. When they finally go to bed together, their love-making is handled dismissively by Fitzgerald, and so it becomes stripped of all feeling. They first drink enough to make themselves feel happy. 'She wanted to be taken and she was, and what had begun with a childish infatuation on a beach was accomplished at last' (p. 233). Their affair ends with Rosemary's tears and accusations, but it fades by mutual consent. Rosemary cannot cope with Dick's bitter possessiveness, preferring her memories of Paris. She now asks him, 'But what have you got for me?' (p. 238).

The movie queen on holiday

Rosemary's final 'scene' in the novel is on the beach. Whereas in Book I it was she who viewed Nicole, now in Book III it is her turn to be viewed through Nicole's critical and hostile eyes. The reversals in the structure of the novel are complete. Nicole recognizes her charm as self-conscious art, yet still remembers the hurt that Rosemary's taking possession of Dick had once caused her: 'the sigh that rocked out of her bosom was something left over from five years ago' (p. 302). Nicole's clinical analysis of the meeting makes it clear that Rosemary is now a movie-star with a public image to maintain. She has an entourage of followers and has no wish to be involved with has-beens. Even while she is talking to Dick, her mind is busy recalling recent gossip that he is no longer socially acceptable: 'He's not received anywhere any more' (p. 308).

Nicole watches Dick exercising the strategies of his charm on Rosemary. This is one of a series of scenes in this part of the novel when Dick invites humiliation. While he puts on a performance for Rosemary's eyes, he fails dismally because as a heavy drinker of thirty-eight he cannot achieve the feat of rising on a water-ski board with a man on his shoulders, something he had easily been able to do two years previously. Nicole is aware that the young men in Rosemary's entourage do not find him interesting and that beneath their polite deference there is an undercurrent of 'Who are these Numbers anyhow?' (p. 304).

Briefly, Dick is surrounded on the beach by the three women who had loved him five years earlier, but who have now all moved away from him.

Nicole's feelings are the most complex and will be discussed later; Mary North can afford to express contempt; Rosemary begins to find him tedious, and as a result covers her embarrassment by asking Topsy if she would like to be an actress one day, only to be publicly snubbed by Nicole.

Nicole still feels a sense of rivalry towards Rosemary, but it is on account of her youth. As a woman of twenty-nine she sees in her the epitome of the cult of youth, a cult encouraged by 'the moving pictures with their myriad faces of girl-children, blandly represented as carrying on the work and wisdom of the world' (p. 312). She is quite indifferent when she guesses that Dick has probably gone off with Rosemary, and tells Tommy Barban: 'Rosemary Hoyt turned up, and either they're together or she upset him so much that he wants to go away and dream about her' (p. 314). When Dick returns the next day, he tells Nicole that he had taken Rosemary to Avignon to put her on the train. He had wanted to see whether there could ever be anything between them, but admits failure: 'Rosemary didn't grow up ... It's probably better that way' (p. 321).

Rosemary thus vanishes from the narrative, dismissed by this final comment from Dick. In Book III the narrative device of focusing on her through Nicole's critical eyes has stripped her of any personal interest, showing her to be a very conventional young woman who is primarily conscious of her public image as a star and who has nothing to offer Dick in the way of a mature relationship. As he says, she has not grown up. Her interest in Book III is in the way she is used to reflect Dick's state of mind and his diminished status. In his desperation he was prepared to use her, but he has to admit that she has nothing to give.

He 'was much admired by the ladies'

In Book II (p. 147), Franz points out to the young Dr Diver that he is most attractive to women. Dick is loved or admired by most of the women in the novel, but he is also exploited and used by them. His deterioration and failure are inextricably linked with his sexual attractiveness to women and his need of their love. The final chapter, with its brief record of Dick's further failures and continued journeying after the end of the main narrative, still implicates women in his life. In Lockport, Nicole is informed, he 'was much admired by the ladies' (Book III, p. 338), but he leaves after being involved in a lawsuit about some medical question and because of an entanglement with a girl working in a grocery store. In Geneva she 'got the impression that he had settled down with some one

75

to keep house for him', but this apparently also does not last. Dick's tragedy continues. As a shell of the man he once was, it seems that he still needs to arouse 'a fascinated and uncritical love' (Book I, p. 36) in women and to exercise 'the old fatal pleasingness, the old forceful charm ... because it had early become a habit to be loved' (Book III, p. 324). But it is no help to him.

Nicole Diver

Nicole is the most important woman in Dick Diver's life, and as such she has been left to the end of this chapter. Her consciousness, both in the rambling free-association monologue which links the two periods of time in Book II and also in the final chapters of Book III, is a major means of reflecting on Dick. Fitzgerald employs the intelligence of someone who is close to Dick to interpret his inner state of mind. Nicole knows, for example, that Dick's bursts of gaiety are followed by periods of depression (Book I, p. 36), and she recognizes towards the end that Dick is immersed in 'his own story spinning out inside him, his own, not hers' (Book III, p. 323). What she never understands is the nature of the guilt and self-recrimination that are tearing him apart, and from which, as the final paragraph of the novel conveys, he is never to recover.

Nicole is handled differently by Fitzgerald from the other women characters. Like the unnamed woman patient in the clinic, she is a victim, both of herself and of circumstances, who arouses pity in Dick; they both appeal to his sympathy and haunt his imagination. But Nicole is an intimate part of Dick's emotional and imaginative life, and he knows that no other woman has shared his most intense experiences as she has done. For him, loving Nicole has been 'a wild submergence of soul, a dipping of all colors into an obscuring dye' (Book II, p. 236). He has cherished Nicole, experienced sexual passion with her and shared little moments of tenderness, such as when she ran barefoot over the wet grass to him and he walked her standing on his feet. While the voice of the narrator handles the other women characters with irony and critical detachment, Nicole is made a much more complex figure. In this novel about a group of rich, egotistical people into whose orbit Dick allows himself to be swept, Nicole takes over his life for ten years, draining him of emotional vitality before she recovers from her crippling mental illness. But she does not simply buy Dick as her sister Baby Warren might have done, she *offers* herself to him in the moonlight (Book II, pp. 152, 171), so that for one moment Dick sees himself 'only as a reflection in her wet eyes'. He surrenders himself to her, merges his identity in hers for one fatal moment, and loses his sense of his independent life and future. In placing her sick self under his cherishing control and care Nicole becomes 'just an image on his mind' (Book III, p. 298), until she asserts her independence by choosing Tommy Barban, a man whose view of life accords more fully with that of her wealthy set. Fitzgerald is critical of Nicole, but he handles her with justice and sympathy.

Three views of Nicole

BOOK I: ROSEMARY'S VIEW

In Book I, until that terrible outburst of 'verbal inhumanity' (p. 125) which forms its climax and end, Nicole is usually a silent, withdrawn figure. The presentation of her is primarily visual; she is perceived through Rosemary's eyes, which are acutely aware of the signs of her wealth. Mrs Speers, who is a good judge of the commercial value of her own daughter's looks, notes that Nicole has the finer bone structure. Yet although Nicole is often silent, she is a loved and respected member of the set, though at one point (p. 29) Rosemary reflects that she wouldn't like to have Nicole as an enemy because she has a sharp tongue (in fact Rosemary is to experience her tongue years later when Nicole snubs her on the beach). What Rosemary notices initially is her 'string of creamy pearls' (pp. 14, 18, 25), her withdrawal from the gaiety, though to the young girl this seems 'a lovely peace' (p. 18), and the vividness of her 'thick, dark, gold hair like a chow's' (pp. 23, 41). In contrast, the narrating voice notes 'the soft gleam of piteous doubt that looked from her green eyes' (p. 34), which is just one instance of the ways in which Rosemary's naïve assumptions are undermined. At the Villa Diana dinner-party Rosemary notices at one point that she is 'still as still' (p. 43). Next she watches her taking a yellow evening bag and 'then sweeping into it all the yellow articles she could find' before pressing it upon Mrs Speers (p. 44). In this section of the novel she is always associated with things – luxury possessions – under Rosemary's fascinated gaze.

In the Paris scenes she is defined, along with Mary North and Rosemary, as being different from 'so many American women' in that 'they preserved their individuality through men and not by opposition to them' (p. 63). All three need men. Rosemary overhears the whispered conversation between husband and wife expressing their sexual need for each other, and wants a sexual adventure with Dick herself. She also shops lavishly with Nicole (pp. 65, 110) and notes that: 'Everything she liked that she couldn't possibly use herself, she bought as a present for a friend' (p. 65).

As the two young women separate Nicole says, 'We had fun, didn't we?' (p. 66). The word 'fun' recurs with increasing irony in the novel, its association with lavish spending becoming clear. Except at the point when the narrative focuses directly on Nicole while she spends her wealth, she is in the background in Book I. But the tension which Dick's obsession with Rosemary arouses in her is apparent in irritable exchanges with Dick at the Gare Saint-Lazare (p. 96) or in the hotel (p. 112). Her explosion of mental illness shocks the reader, but Fitzgerald has already conveyed that she is under acute stress.

BOOK II – 'THE YOUNG BIRD WITH WINGS CRUSHED SOMEHOW': DICK'S VIEW

Nicole's neurosis is diagnosed in specialist terms by the psychiatrists in Dr Dohmler's clinic ('Divided Personality. Acute and down-hill phase of the illness. The fear of men is a symptom of the illness and is not at all constitutional' (p. 143)), and Franz describes her 'transference'[2] to Dick as the best thing that could have happened to her, but in general Fitzgerald deliberately rejected the use of psychiatric detail, writing in his Notebook: 'Only suggest from the most remote facts. *Not* like doctors' stories.'[3] The novel is about Dick Diver's tragedy, not Nicole's illness.

Dick is delighted to watch the young Nicole finding pleasure in her own femininity, the way she pauses in front of a mirror 'so that the incorruptible quicksilver could give her back to herself' (p. 153), but he also recognizes early on his own central role in this: 'the difficulty was that, eventually, Nicole brought everything to his feet, gifts of sacrificial ambrosia, of worshipping myrtle' (p. 153). It is difficult to judge exactly what these metaphors imply. In worshipping him Nicole is offering herself to him, but in his awareness her beauty is enhanced by her wealth: she is 'beautiful and rich' (p. 153). Fitzgerald never overstates her allure, but his choice of language and imagery in the flashback scenes acts as a reminder that Nicole is wealthy as well as fragile, beautiful and appealing. Dick knows that Franz and Dr Dohmler are right in advising him not to 'devote half your life to being doctor and nurse and all' (p. 156), but he cannot resist that conjunction of qualities in Nicole, together with the effect of moonlight on his senses and imagination.

The adverse effects, after 1925, of feeling herself constrained by Dick and by living in the clinic are conveyed with great economy through Dick's responses to them: 'Often he felt lonely with her, and frequently she tired him' (p. 206). When she runs away from him 'secretly' at the fair her relapse is recounted by means of one brilliant image: in her yellow dress she is 'an ochre stitch along the edge of reality and unreality' (p. 207).

When she becomes a 'grinning mask' which he wants to smash to a jelly (p. 211), the violence in both of them is destructive. Nicole's outbreak is the catalyst that drives Dick away on his disastrous travels at the conclusion of Book II.

BOOK III: NICOLE'S VIEW OF HERSELF

Nicole is given prominence in Book III when her consciousness is employed as the location of the narrative. At the beginning of the book Kaethe Gregorovious, who has always felt inferior to her, makes a harsh judgement which may, however, have some truth in it: 'I think Nicole is less sick than any one thinks – she only cherishes her illness as an instrument of power' (p. 259).

Once they are back on the Riviera, Nicole accuses Dick of wanting to smash things up. It is she who takes the lead now, saying that they cannot go on as they are. She tells Dick: 'Some of the time I think it's my fault – I've ruined you' (p. 287). She is alarmed and, later, on Golding's yacht, terrified by his reaction to her suggestion that he is 'ruined', and for one moment thinks he is going to kill himself and her (p. 294). But the next morning she begins to enjoy the rivalry between Tommy Barban and her husband. She can now cherish her sexual power, not the power of her illness: 'other women have lovers – why not me? . . . Why shouldn't I?' (p. 297). When Dick, recognizing what has happened, retires to lie down on his bed, Nicole is 'aware of the sin she had committed against him' (p. 300).

Fitzgerald is fair to Nicole in tracing her state of mind. She has a sense of moral responsibility, but the narrating voice makes the suggestion that, as she reverts to her own identity, the influence of her wealth becomes uppermost: 'Nicole had been designed for change, for flight, with money as fins and wings' (p. 301).

The years of courtesy, style, politeness with Dick have now become irksome to her, and Tommy Barban's more brutal personality with its promise of unrestrained sexuality is attractive. He makes no moral demands on her and accepts her 'white crook's eyes' (p. 314) as he accepts her wealth. Being with him seems to release her from all the moral constraints of her life with Dick: 'New vistas appeared ahead, peopled with the faces of many men, none of whom she need obey or even love' (p. 315). When they make love in the cheap hotel room, Fitzgerald uses the image of her struggling 'like a decapitated animal' (p. 316) to convey her total physical abandonment. The irruption into their room of the two American girls, 'young, thin and barbaric' (p. 319), adds a touch of irony to the end of Nicole's love scene. As the girls follow the fleet, one of them waves goodbye with her panties. The star-spangled banner and the waving panties signal the triumph of a brash new America over Dick's old one: 'Moment by moment all that Dick had taught her fell away ... Tangled with love in the moonlight she welcomed the anarchy of her lover' (p. 320).

Nicole has to force herself to challenge Dick in order to make a break with him. 'With the opportunistic memory of women' (p. 322) she begins to push to the back of her mind all the accumulated memories of ten years of marriage and the passion they have shared. She knows that the influence of Dick's intelligence has always required honesty of her, 'substrata of truth under truth' (p. 323), and the weapon she fights with is the knowledge of the power of her wealth, 'the plush arrogance of a top dog' (p. 324):

she fought him with her money and her faith that her sister disliked him and was behind her now; with the thought of the new enemies he was making with his bitterness, with her quick guile against his wine-ing and dine-ing slowness, her health and beauty against his physical deterioration, her unscrupulousness against his moralities ... Then she walked, weak in the legs, and sobbing coolly, toward the household that was hers at last [p. 324].

Fitzgerald sums up a great deal of Nicole's inner stress in this short paragraph because its real importance is the light it reflects not only on Dick's isolation, but also on his moral integrity. However, it ensures that Nicole is given identity as a woman of feeling, even though her sobbing is now 'cool'. The final chapter of the novel recording Dick's subsequent history has the same double function.

5. The Structure of *Tender is the Night*

I would like to say in regard to my book that there was a deliberate intention in every part of it except the first [Book I]. The first part, the romantic introduction, was too long and too elaborated largely because of the fact that it had been written over a series of years with varying plans, but everything else in the book conformed to a *definite intention* and if I had to write it again tomorrow I would adopt the same plan . . .[1]

Whether or not the reader agrees with his strictures about Book I, Fitzgerald's defence of the novel offers a clear pronouncement on his intentions while writing it. I have tried to show throughout this study that the complex time-scheme of the novel is an essential part of its aesthetic structure. The discussion in this chapter will focus on other features of the narrative structure which contribute to the artistic unity of the novel. In the letter quoted Fitzgerald is alluding to criticism of the way the narrative distances Dick Diver at the end, so that he fades from the text as a diminishing object in Nicole's memory. (This has already been discussed on p. 52.) He fades into time as well as space: the reader is aware that the action is all over. A careful reading of the first paragraph will show that this is implicit here, rendering Dick Diver's failure, isolation and exclusion from the beach he has made fashionable and from all that he has loved more final and desolating. The links between the first and last paragraphs create a symmetry which is characteristic of the novel:

On the pleasant shore of the French Riviera, about half way between Marseilles and the Italian border, stands a large, proud, rose-colored hotel. Deferential palms cool its flushed façade, and before it stretches a short dazzling beach. *Lately* it has become a summer resort of notable and fashionable people; *a decade ago* it was almost deserted after its English clientele went north in April. *Now*, many bungalows cluster near it, *but when this story begins* only the cupolas of a dozen old villas rotted like water lilies among the massed pines between Gausse's Hôtel des Étrangers and Cannes, five miles away [Book I, p. 11; italics mine].

The contrasts between 'lately' and 'a decade ago' in one sentence and 'now' and 'but when this story begins' in the next emphasize the passing of time as well as the speed of fashionable change. There was also a time prior to 'when this story begins' when there were no foreigners there at all in the summer months, and only wealthy Britons in the winter. It is now Americans who dominate that 'large, proud, rose-colored hotel' where even the palm-trees are 'deferential'. The Divers, we learn, are responsible for creating the summer season.

The importance of the time-scheme in the organization of the novel has been discussed in Chapter 2. As a major feature of the narrative structure, the handling of time controls the representation of character, and shapes the reader's emotional responses to Dick Diver. Time is, in effect, psychological as well as chronological in the selective use Fitzgerald makes of it, in the way he gives considerable emotional value to particular moments while passing over periods of years elsewhere. Essentially, *Tender is the Night* is a psychological novel, making its effect through the varying tones which suggest the moods and subjective worlds of the three main characters. For this reason the sequence of their points of view, briefly referred to already on p. 40, is a major feature of the structure, one that will be discussed in this chapter. In the novel Fitzgerald combines very realistic dialogue with a sharply incisive use of language to convey with detachment and an edge of irony particular qualities of a scene or a character. This is true even of his representation of Dick Diver: the reader is required to judge him as well as sympathize with him. But there is another level of language of a lyrical or poetic kind which, in the early part of the novel, conveys intense moments of ecstasy when characters momentarily lose the consciousness of self and their separate identity. Since Dick's increasing sense of alienation from himself and from society becomes the main process of the narrative, such moments of ecstatic communication are confined to the first half of the novel.

Although the novel is organized into three books, it falls into two halves linked by Nicole's rambling free-association monologue (Book II, pp. 175–9; see also the chart on p. 35 in this study). Her speech is directed at no one, and it briefly puts the reader into the role of a psychoanalyst, listening with detachment and making the connecting links about the emotional and moral pressures on Dick during the six years of his marriage between 1919 and 1925. With this section dividing them, the two halves exist in a mirror relationship effected by the taut, tightly controlled structure. By cutting factual information to a minimum, conveying it instead through characters' consciousness, Fitzgerald is able to handle events selectively and shape them into a pattern. The basic structure of the novel consists of contrast and opposition. Scenes in the second half of the novel reflect back on others in the first half to create a contrast of mood which reveals the characters' psychological separation from their earlier selves. The relationship between Dick and Nicole Diver is the foundation upon which the oppositions exist. As she recovers, she needs him less and less: as he suffers increasingly from a sense of moral guilt at his enjoyment of her world of wealth, he can help her less. As Nicole finds her old identity and achieves a sense of a unified self, Dick loses his. In committing incest with her father, the adolescent Nicole had experienced such guilt that she subsequently cut herself off by illness from the community of the new America created by her millionaire family: Book III relates her successful reintegration into it. Dick comes to realize in Book II that by marrying Nicole he has cut himself off from the traditional values of his father and the old American community: in Book III he is preparing to try to reintegrate himself into it as Dr Diver, but the final paragraph implies his failure.

As the fundamental opposition of needs and interests between Dick and Nicole becomes clear to the reader, it also becomes evident that Dick has been aware of this since the summer of 1925, that key point in the novel. Fitzgerald does not state this but lets the growing conflict between them at the end of Book II and the beginning of Book III bring it to a head. However, to a certain extent this is already prefigured in Book I, where the recurrence of violence and death is important as a structural device, conveying a sense of suppressed tension that undercuts the seemingly happy relationships and emphasizes characters' psychological insecurity. In Book I violence and aggression seem hardly to touch the main characters; in Book II Nicole's violence is an unavoidable symptom of her schizophrenic state; but later in Book II the violence is located in Dick himself, reaching its climax in Book III when Nicole, 'Cold with terror' (p. 294), fears he will destroy them both. Dick controls his aggression by effecting an emotional withdrawal from their shared life. The way in which the exterior aggression of the first half is internalized in Dick Diver in the second is an example of Fitzgerald's brilliant control of narrative structure.

The function of violence, death and aggression in the novel

There is a scene of potential violence early in Book I when Tommy Barban feels called upon to protect the privacy of the Divers from the gossiping tongue of Violet McKisko and challenges Albert McKisko to a duel (Chapters IX–XI). Whatever it was that Violet McKisko saw in the bathroom of Villa Diana is unknown to the reader and also to Rosemary Hoyt at this point. The duel, handled as comedy, is presented through the eyes of an outsider who does not know what is going on and only learns of it by chance. Rather incongruously, Albert McKisko emerges as a 'hero', very much raised in his self-esteem. He has to get himself drunk before his ordeal, and is saved because Abe North insists on forty paces between the combatants. The affair verges on the ludicrous, and yet it serves to mark the end of a seemingly idyllic period of summer and harmony that reached its climax at the Villa Diana dinner-party. This, followed by the trip to the trenches, is a prelude to the break-up of the party of friends.

The two deaths in Book I also serve to darken the tone of this summer period. In fact, they bring it to a close. Abe North's supposed departure for New York to resume his musical career is accompanied by murder. The murder of a man, presumably her lover, by Maria Wallis, an American acquaintance of the Divers, is a purely fortuitous occurrence, but it adds strangeness and tension to an already strained scene. Abe is desperate for a drink and feeling disagreeable; Nicole is preoccupied; all the women are oppressed by Abe's mood and dependent on Dick, needing him to manage the situation for them. Once the shots have been fired, however, Dick feels himself losing control of everyone. Both Nicole and Rosemary, who are aware of their rivalry over him, seem to challenge his male authority, perhaps as Maria Wallis has just done in her relationship. Fitzgerald stresses the effect on them:

> However, everything had happened – Abe's departure and Mary's impending departure for Salzburg this afternoon had ended the time in Paris. Or perhaps the shots, the concussions that had finished God knew what dark matter, had terminated it. The shots had entered into all their lives: echoes of violence followed them out onto the pavement ... [p. 97]

The snatch of gossip from the porters which ends the chapter emphasizes the ugliness of the scene: one of them says that the little luxury revolver has drawn so much blood it's like being back in the war.

The death of Jules Peterson is also tangential, yet it creates repercussions in the lives of Dick, Nicole and Rosemary (Book I, Chapters XXIV–XXV). Abe, who seems to be permanently drunk and a bore to his friends on his return to Paris, wrongly identifies a man to the police as the one who, he claims, stole a thousand-franc note from him. He is supported by Peterson, who is down on his luck and anxious for some financial help, and he brings the man to the hotel to enlist Dick's interest. Peterson is murdered as an act of revenge and left on Rosemary's bed. Rosemary's reputation must be preserved at all costs, and Dick acts with his customary efficiency to protect her. He gets Nicole to exchange one of their bed-spreads for Rosemary's and dumps Peterson in the corridor, before telephoning the hotel detective. Dick's charm does not fail him, since he has already made a friend of the latter. Not only is Rosemary's reputation at stake, but so is that of a great hotel, and money and influence easily effect a discreet end to the affair. Peterson, the victim of this sordid little matter initiated by Abe, is too insignificant to matter. He becomes simply 'the remains' (p. 125), quickly disposed of. Although Dick is not personally implicated, his integrity does seem to be in question, since he is ready to let money pervert the facts. He is involved in the repercussions, too, since Nicole breaks down under the strain of the sight of the blood-stained coverlet and blames him. Fitzgerald makes her screams the climax of the Paris holiday. His use of language deliberately dehumanizes Nicole: she becomes simply a source of noise for the horrified listener, 'a verbal inhumanity' that sweeps into the hotel suite and 'in the shape of horror took form again' (p. 125). The powerful associations of blood have threatened her insecure sense of herself as a woman, and she retreats into insanity.

The flashback sequence at the beginning of Book II places her in an ambivalent light which is sustained all through the novel. The young and fragile Nicole is herself a source of violence and aggression, which seems to be sexual in origin. In 1918 her first letters to Dick (Book II, pp. 136–9) are described as of 'a marked pathological turn' (p. 135), by which Fitzgerald implies that they are the neurotic outpourings of a sick mind. These rambling letters make reference to patients being bound by belts and to her own attempt to attack a man in a sweet-shop.

Much more of a shock to the reader is Nicole's last outbreak in 1928 (?) because her violence seems to be malevolent (Book II, pp. 206–12). As always, any emotional strain brings back her schizophrenia: the letter from a recently discharged patient accusing Dick of seducing her daughter reawakens Nicole's old jealousy and is enough to demolish her precariously maintained stability: ' "Home!" she roared in a voice so abandoned that its louder tones wavered and cracked. "And sit and think that we're all rotting and the children's ashes are rotting in every box I open? That filth!" ' (p. 209). As soon as she sees the signs of emotional withdrawal in Dick's face she becomes immediately dependent on him, begging for help. But this is not the end of the matter. She is totally unpredictable in this state, and laughs – 'hilariously, unashamed, unafraid, unconcerned' (p. 211) – when she tries to destroy them all by steering the car over the mountainside.

The casually reported death of Abe North soon after this seems to set in train further acts of violence as the tone of the novel becomes increasingly sombre. Abe has been battered to death in a New York bar (Book II, p. 218), and Dick's pent-up feelings burst out as he recognizes the parallels in their two lives of initial promise followed by failure and deterioration. Fitzgerald deliberately places Dick within the frame of a universal grief as he grieves alone in his hotel room, for outside the German town honours its dead of the First World War:

> It was a society of veterans going to lay wreaths on the tombs of the dead. The column marched slowly with a sort of swagger for a lost magnificence, a past effort, a forgotten sorrow. The faces were only formally sad but Dick's lungs burst for a moment with regret for Abe's death, and his own youth of ten years ago [p. 219].

Abe's futile death sums up the futility of his final years. His wasted talents, his alcoholism and his pursuit of folly and humiliation are defined on p. 94 as 'a will to die'. Freud developed the concept of a death-wish as the contrary impulse to the sexual energy which supports the life instincts. The death-wish is a form of self-destructive energy, and Dick's self-destructive impulses at the end of Book II, by which point he is impelled to bring about his own humiliation and punishment in Rome, mirror those of Abe. Both of them are victims of themselves and of the post-war feelings of despair. As Nicole had said of Abe in Paris (Book I, p. 112): 'So many smart men go to pieces nowadays.' Thus, later scenes bring a new dimension of meaning to words spoken casually in the first half.

Dick's sombre mood is deepened when the telegram announcing his father's death in New York reaches him soon afterwards (Book II, p. 222). The death of a loved figure who provided him with the basic values of his life forces him to take stock of himself. He feels he has betrayed those values of a gentleman by which his father had lived a quiet and honourable life. He has broken with the traditions of his heritage: 'These dead, he knew them all, their weather-beaten faces with blue flashing eyes, the spare violent bodies, the souls made of new earth in the forest-heavy darkness of the seventeenth century' (p. 224). The traditional moral integrity valued by the founding fathers of the American nation in the seventeenth century is not proof against the modern greedy and aggressive world, and he personally has betrayed it.

After his unsatisfactory affair with Rosemary in Rome, Dick's frustration breaks out in a mindless outburst of rage against the Romans, though it is really himself he is attacking. Just as Abe had sought to punish himself, so Dick does too. Drunk and spoiling for a fight, he hits out at a policeman over the trivial matter of a taxi fare and smashes him to the ground:

> For a moment he stood over him in savage triumph – but even as a first pang of doubt shot through him the world reeled; he was clubbed down, and fists and boots beat on him in a savage tattoo. He felt his nose break like a shingle and his eyes jerk as if they had snapped back on a rubber band into his head. A rib splintered under a stamping heel [p. 246].

The reprisal is clearly vindictive, and yet the style does not create sympathy for Dick, only horror at the brutality. It is such a new turn in events for him to be personally involved in mindless violence that the contrast with the Dick Diver of Book I is disturbing, and his deterioration in this scene is thus rendered all the more dramatic. The remainder of this situation is handled as semi-comedy through the person of Baby Warren. She becomes the star figure who bullies American officials to obtain Dick's release. Yet, overall, the effect is not comic, since Dick is morally culpable. He is even mistaken for a child rapist and murderer by the crowd, who hiss and boo him, their 'voices full of fury and scorn' (p. 255). To punish himself even further, Dick says: 'I want to make a speech . . . I want to explain to these people how I raped a five-year-old girl. Maybe I did' (p. 256). Child rape has ugly implications: it reflects back on that taboo incident of Devereux Warren's incestuous relationship with his adolescent daughter, Nicole. Dick, who has become an authority (father) figure for Nicole as well as her lover/husband, is unconsciously punishing himself for this. Thus, events in the second half again create various threads of psychological interest which are linked with earlier scenes.

Episodes of violence or death intrude increasingly upon Dick's life until aggression becomes a facet of his own behaviour at the end of Book II. The language with which Fitzgerald presents these creates a series of images which establish a deepening sense of loss and desperation in him. Most of the settings, too, contribute towards the creation of particular moods, and function to distinguish the two halves of the book.

The contribution of settings to mood in the first half of the novel

Light permeates the opening sequences of Book I and the flashback section at the beginning of Book II. For instance, the second paragraph of the novel vividly creates a world of sensuous appeal and suggests a particular place possessing its own style of beauty, colour and effects of light:

The hotel and its bright tan prayer rug of a beach were one. In the early morning the distant image of Cannes, the pink and cream of old fortifications, the purple Alp that bounded Italy, were cast across the water and lay quavering in the ripples and rings sent up by sea-plants through the clear shallows. Before eight a man came down to the beach in a blue bathrobe and with much preliminary application to his person of the chilly water, and much grunting and loud breathing, floundered a minute in the sea. When he had gone, beach and bay were quiet for an hour. Merchantmen crawled westward on the horizon; bus boys shouted in the hotel court; the dew dried upon the pines. In another hour the horns of motors began to blow down from the winding road along the low range of the Maures, which separates the littoral [the shore] from true Provençal France [Book I, p. 11].

The effect is of harmony: architecturally, past and present blend; the setting frames the human beings in a peace that is not desecrated by noise or discord or disruption. Nothing jars the scene. When Rosemary first goes into the water the language used is again sensuous, deliberately conveying a safe pastoral world of union between human beings and the elements: 'The water reached up for her, pulled her down tenderly out of the heat, seeped in her hair and ran into the corners of her body' (p. 13). As she rests after this she lies listening to 'the small exhausted wa-*waa* of the expiring waves' (p. 14). To Rosemary's sleepy gaze even the town of Cannes, five miles away, seems 'faded to a mirage of what was fresh and cool; a robin-breasted sailing boat pulled in behind it a strand from the outer, darker sea' (p. 19). The author's concern here is with the effects of a harmonious scene upon a mind relaxed and at peace with itself; the choice of 'robin-breasted' rather than 'red' contributes to that sense of a world which carries no threat. When Rosemary eats her late lunch with her mother, their table is crossed by the flickering patterns of light and shade made by the pine trees outside.

Fitzgerald creates few such effects in the final chapters of the Divers' return to the Riviera in Book III. For one thing, the idyllic pastoral world has been destroyed, and more important, none of the characters is in a mood or a position to respond to such quiet, sensuous beauty.

Moonlight contributes to the atmosphere during the Divers' dinner-party at the Villa Diana (Book I, pp. 37–48), aptly named, as Diana was ➤ the goddess of the moon. All the guests are transfixed momentarily in the magic provided by the Divers' social expertise. But the magic, all too brief, is more than the product of charm. All of them are responsive to the night, the vastness of the universe, the Mediterranean far below them. The mood is initially created by the innocent childish voices of the little boy and girl singing *'Au clair de la lune'*, a traditional song of moonlight and longing for the unattainable. The guests experience 'a sense of being alone with each other in the dark universe' (p. 44), and 'the soft-pawed night and the ghostly wash of the Mediterranean far below' suffuses all of them. It cannot last, however. Immediately after this Nicole disappears, to be followed by Violet McKisko in prosaic and determined search of the bathroom, which results in the disquieting comedy of the duel and the breaking up of the charmed circle of friends.

Rosemary's readiness to be charmed also contributes to her impression of Paris as a city of lights, colours and changing moods in the first half of the novel: 'The river shimmered with lights from the bridges and cradled many cold moons' (p. 70). She enjoys the experience of crossing Paris before dawn on a wagon piled high with carrots for the vegetable market. With 'the warm darkness streaming down' around her, she is aware of the 'earth in the carrot beards ... fragrant and sweet' (p. 90). Never again is she so relaxed, spontaneous and innocent as she is at this moment of self-forgetfulness.

The responses of youth are also important in the flashback sequence of Dick's initial meetings with Nicole and her expropriation of him (Book II, pp. 157–61). The two of them are suffused with moonlight in the solitude. For Dick, Nicole seems to take her fragile identity from the flickering effects of light and shade, and his sense of her vulnerability is intensified. The way in which Fitzgerald blends the effects of this on Dick's sensibility with the effects on both of them of tinny jazz heard against the vast backdrop of a Swiss mountain has already been discussed. Nicole knows how to exploit her own sexuality but the sense of their communion is created by moonlight, their isolation and the grandeur of this towering world around them.

In the chapter following this, when Dick meets the liberated Nicole with her bobbed hair in the resort above Montreux (Book II, pp. 165–72), their youthful sense of the freshness of life is completed by flowers. Nicole is often associated with flowers. 'Dorothy Perkins roses' force their way into each compartment of the funicular (p. 164), and the car passes a hill 'solid with narcissus, from passengers to sky' (p. 165). After Nicole has kissed Dick under the stars shimmering 'through the white crests of the high Alps' (p. 169), she speaks of having already offered herself to him like flowers: 'I can remember how I stood waiting for you in the garden – holding all my self in my arms like a basket of flowers. It was that to me anyhow – I thought I was sweet – waiting to hand that basket to you' (p. 172).

Fitzgerald achieves effects of lyrical emotion experienced through the youthful consciousness of the characters in the first half of the novel. These scenes impress themselves strongly on the reader's memory as a contrast to the rapid accumulation in the second half of scenes of egotism and humiliation which precede Dick's renunciation of everything. Innocence in the first half of the novel is contrasted with experience in the second. For example, in the beach episodes in Book III, the characters are self-consciously attempting studied effects, and 'few people swam any more in that blue paradise' (p. 302). This acts as a direct reference back to the sensuous pleasure Rosemary had enjoyed in the sea at the beginning of the novel. Another example of verbal echoes creating contrasts with earlier moments of experience is to be found when Nicole spends the night with Tommy Barban in a cheap shore hotel. She is described as 'tangled with moonlight', and the implications of assertive sexuality are reinforced by imagery of 'anarchy', 'swords' and 'wolfed' (p. 320). Reference to moonlight picks up the earlier imagery of moonlight when Dick first kissed her, but the sense of merging with or losing one's identity in the identity of the other is lost. In this scene she asserts hers.

Before examining other episodes in the second half of the novel in which a deliberately harsh contrast is achieved with those moments in the first where the sensuous beauty of refracted sunlight, moonlight in vast open spaces or the scent of flowers finds a response in the consciousness of the onlooker, it is worth considering the title of the novel. The quotation from Keats's 'Ode to a Nightingale' in the title draws attention to a particular quality of emotion and gives it value. It is an emotion which belongs only to the first half of the novel.

The title of the novel

The implications of the earlier, discarded titles, *The Drunkard's Holiday* and *Dr Diver's Holiday*, are obvious: the former puts the emphasis on the second half of the novel and on Dick's alcoholism, while the latter puts the emphasis on his ambition to be 'a good psychologist – maybe to be the greatest one that ever lived' (Book II, p. 147). In either case, the word 'holiday' contributes a note of irony, conveying that Dick's life among the very wealthy is an interim and also that it is a putting aside of his real life. In his final choice of title Fitzgerald changed the whole emphasis.

A tribute is paid to Keats in Book II when Dick, disillusioned and despairing, walks to the Spanish Steps in Rome and 'his spirit soared before the flower stalls and the house where Keats had died' (p. 240). By employing Keats's 'Ode to a Nightingale'[2] for both the title and the epigraph of his novel, Fitzgerald draws the emotional experience of the poem into Dick's experience. The poem evokes a warm summer evening suffused with the scent of roses and the song of the nightingale. In the novel, in scenes which recall the poem, the plangent notes of popular music or of a children's melody replace the song of the bird in stirring the emotions. In the Ode, during the brief moment of harmony in which the scene fuses with his own emotions, the poet expresses a desire to submerge his own consciousness, his sense of his own separate identity, in the magic of universal timelessness that the scene evokes, and briefly feels that he has achieved this:

> Already with thee! tender is the night,
>   . . . But here there is no light,
>   Save what from heaven is with the breezes blown
>   Through verdurous glooms and winding mossy ways.

However, the moment is transient; the poet knows it cannot last, and has to acknowledge the reality of a world of pain, suffering and death from which there is no escape. By the end of the poem the bird's song is fading fast and the poet is left wondering about the actuality of the experience. By using his powers of language to evoke that languorous evening full of scents and sound and the mystery of changing lights and shadows, Keats makes the experience of romantic longing an important feature in human life, while recognizing that it can only be transient and perhaps is only a dream. By yielding to the night and the moonlight and to Nicole's passionate love for himself, together with the glamour of her money, Dick tries to perpetuate that romantic moment of the 'wild submergence of soul' (Book II, p. 236). He immerses himself in a dream which becomes a nightmare for him; his independence as a man whose work can give meaning to his life is destroyed.

The capacity to surrender oneself to a moment of magic is associated with youth in the novel: Dick, Nicole and Rosemary are all young in the flashback sequence and in Book I. However, when Rosemary experiences ecstasy at the Villa Diana dinner-party, Dick has become a charming manipulator of people and moods, contriving the magic almost by a series of tricks to display the power of his personality and virtuosity. Although this does not show until the second half of Book II, he is about to begin the restless emotional journey which brings him to a point of alienation from society and from himself, as those final postmarks from ever smaller towns in New York State at the very end of the novel testify. It is the 'tenderness of the night' during those scenes in the flashback sequence which gives Dick's journey into despair its particular poignancy. Fitzgerald thus employs the associative power of Keats's poem and in addition weights those early scenes in the novel with a particular quality of romantic emotion in order to validate the idealistic and imaginative desire of youth to find a union which transcends self. Romantic love seeks an ideal, but in the second half of the novel there is no place for idealism.

The process of dehumanization in the second half of the novel

The choice of scenes for discussion in this chapter cannot be comprehensive; they are offered as examples of the way in which the organization of the narrative creates two distinct ranges of feeling, those of hope and generous impulse in the first half and those of despair and egotism in the second. Yet, as has been suggested in earlier chapters, Book I also creates a disturbing undercurrent of tension, uncertainty and guilt which keeps threatening to disturb the elegant surface of life, and finally does with Nicole's inhuman screams at the climax of the book. Before looking at episodes in the second half which reflect back as a contrast upon those scenes in the first characterized by light and sensuous pleasure, an examination of Fitzgerald's language describing the battlefield (Book I, pp. 66–70) will show that it already creates particular implications which become obvious in the second half. The 'great funeral pyres' (p. 68) of weapons stand close to the 'great sea of graves'. The weapons are durable reminders of the terrible war, but the dead men are pursuing 'their eternal dissolution' (p. 70): the identities which once distinguished them – Prussian Guards, Old Etonians, Manchester mill hands – are non-existent. The men are represented by things now, in this process of dehumanization which the war has set in motion. In the second half of the novel, Dick, who had aspired to be a great psychologist dedicating his care, intellect and imagination to the cure of mentally shattered human beings, cracks under the strain of self-accusation and bitterness. In the scenes to be discussed below the language associates Dick with dehumanization: Nicole becomes an object for him; he is prepared to use Rosemary as one; in the final episode in Rome he himself becomes one. His earlier idealism, conveyed through images of light, has been lost.

The episode of the recurrence of Nicole's schizophrenia (Book II, pp. 206–12) recalls an earlier scene. The garish fairground setting and the 'sound of a whining, tinkling hootchy-kootchy show' (p. 207) is a grotesque contrast to their evening together in the first half of the novel listening to jazz records, when Nicole's suppressed excitement had seemed to Dick 'to reflect all the excitement of the world' (p. 151). Now, ten years later, Dick is exhausted by his relationship with Nicole – 'that of the husband, that of the psychiatrist' (p. 207) – while Nicole veers unpredictably between aggression and total dependence on him, draining both his resources of love and his capacity for clinical detachment. He is too close emotionally to her to be dispassionate, and cannot 'watch her disintegrations without participating in them' (p. 209). On the way home, while he is reflecting on the struggle ahead to keep her in touch with reality, Nicole tries to steer the car, with their two frightened children in the back, over the edge of the mountain. For Dick she suddenly becomes 'the mad hand clutching the steering wheel' (p. 211) which he has to crush in order to prevent her from destroying them all. When she jeers at him for wanting to live, he finds her 'grinning mask' almost intolerable and desires to smash it. He has to exert all the strength of his personality to control her and himself while trying to maintain a semblance of normality in front of the children and the local men who come to help. The implications in this scene of the unremitting strains on Dick create an immense distance between this period of his life and the early moments of tenderness and shared emotion in the flashback sequence at the beginning of Book II.

The scenes in Rome at the end of Book II (pp. 226–56) offer a very dark reflection of the Paris scenes in Book I. Whereas, then, Dick had gently refused Rosemary's naïve invitation, now he pursues her because he needs to reinforce his own ego; while, in Paris, Abe North's drunken games had seemed unimportant, now Dick's drunken activities reveal his deterioration and self-disgust. Then, Dick was the controller of the group's gaiety; now he is alone and depressed. Meeting Rosemary again, he finds 'eternal moonlight' (p. 230) in her face. As Rosemary has just evaded sexual intercourse, claiming that it would be dangerous because she has no wish to become pregnant, and as immediately afterwards she walks to the mirror to rearrange her hair (she is the same old Rosemary), it would seem that Dick is trying to recapture the old emotional rapture, when in fact all he feels is sexual desire. The phrase 'eternal moonlight' is thus rather puzzling. They are lying on the bed in her hotel room and Dick has rolled over on his back to lift Rosemary above him. She is therefore poised above him like a film-star in close-up, and he is looking up at her face, noticing her slightly chapped lips but trying to re-create the romantic aura of the past which he had experienced with Nicole. He recognizes, however, that he is merely being self-indulgent: Rosemary means nothing to him:

> Dick's discovery that he was not in love with her, nor she with him, had added to rather than diminished his passion for her. Now that he knew he would not enter further into her life, she became the strange woman for him. He supposed many men meant no more than that when they said they were in love – not a wild submergence of soul, a dipping of all colors into an obscuring dye, such as his love for Nicole had been (p. 236).

By that time the 'childish infatuation on a beach [has been] accomplished at last' (p. 233). The game which they had started in Paris now means no more to them than casual sex in a hotel room.

The early scenes in Paris and these later ones in Rome all take place at night, but they are contrasted in detail and mood. In Rome Dick walks through the foul tunnel up to the Spanish Steps (Book II, p. 240), or rides in a taxi 'along cheerless streets through a dank November night. There were no women in the streets, only pale men with dark coats buttoned to the neck, who stood in groups beside shoulders of cold stone' (p. 241). It is actually the Rome of Mussolini, but few overtly political factors enter this novel. When Dick has his disastrous encounter with the taxi-drivers who want to overcharge the wealthy drunken American, the setting is one of 'dirty water in the gutters and between the rough cobblestones; a marshy vapor from the Campagna, a sweat of exhausted cultures [tainting] the morning air' (p. 244). There is nothing tender about the night in the scenes of the second half of the novel. In the first half – up to Nicole's monologue – the rapture experienced by characters is intensified by moonlight and by a sense of communion with each other in a universe which is vast and mysterious. Here, Rome is denoted by its cold stone statuary rather than by the warm earthy fragrance of new carrots; by lonely muffled men and prostitutes rather than by companionship and laughter.

The central argument in this chapter is that the narrative structure is based upon contrast and opposition. The two major settings in the novel, Switzerland and the Riviera, sustain this feature.

Switzerland and the Riviera

In its use of contrast, the structuring of scenes and settings in the novel reflects the opposing personalities and needs of Dick and Nicole. Seemingly so closely bound to each other that in Book I they are known affectionately to their friends as Dicole, they are in fact diametrically opposed in their needs. The two major locations in the novel, the Riviera beach and Switzerland, represent the success or failure of each of them in finding their identity. This is not to say that the settings are metaphors. On the contrary, Fitzgerald makes them accurate representations of the social life of the 1920s, but he also gives these settings symbolic significance in the psychological experience of Dick and Nicole.

Both Swiss clinics represent places of actual incarceration for Nicole. They may be a refuge, but they employ belts and bars and isolation when necessary. Even when she is there as Dick's wife and investor in the clinic, Nicole is still a patient. Yet for Dick the mountains symbolize the isolation in which he might have dedicated himself to work as he had in Vienna, 'with the fine quiet of the scholar which is nearest of all things to heavenly peace' (Book II, p. 130). When the young Dick says that he has only one plan, and that is to be a good psychologist – 'maybe ... the greatest one that ever lived' (p. 147) – Franz finds this a typically American remark, one that could only have been made by someone from a country lacking a great and heroic tradition of intellectuals and thinkers stretching back to the Reformation. Dick admits that he 'was only talking big'. At the point of young Dick's introduction into the novel in the flashback section, Fitzgerald deliberately invokes one of the shaping figures of American history, General Grant, waiting to play his role in the Civil War, though he points out rather enigmatically that the reader of history knows what Grant's destiny was to be. By winning the battle of Vicksburg for the North in the American Civil War, Grant not only mounted one of the boldest campaigns of the war, he made a decisive contribution to the defeat of the South. He was later made President of the United States, though he achieved no glory then. The implication seems to be that Dick's destiny is in the balance when he leaves the army: he has the chance to become a leading American figure in the field of psychiatry. But with a fine edge of irony, Fitzgerald makes Dick's first move in the very next chapter his visit to Dr Dohmler's clinic to inquire about the touching young girl patient he has met on a previous occasion. Dick's destiny, which might have been to find fulfilment of his ambition in Switzerland, is to become a puppet of the Warren wealth and the Warren women.

In Book I the Riviera beach is given attributes of beauty and harmony. There are signs that this will not last – the presence of the social climbers eager to copy the Divers makes this clear. To Rosemary's charmed gaze Dick's activities represent glamour and charm. Later, in Paris, his casual reference to giving up his scientific work is the first hint she has of his medical career. By 1925 he has already had some success with his first little volume, *A Psychology for Psychiatrists* (Book II, p. 182), and he has the materials for the sequel laid out in his workroom at the Villa Diana. Switzerland, the home of Jung, one of the great formative psychologists of this modern science, should have been the scene of Dick's study and application. Instead, while he wastes his life in the playground of the wealthy and frivolous, the Riviera, Dick knows that dedicated and patient men working in libraries will easily get ahead of him. What is more, he is conscious of his own wasted talents and time: 'he felt a discrepancy between the growing luxury in which the Divers lived, and the need for display which apparently went along with it' (p. 182). He lessens the strain on his nerves resulting from helping Nicole through the late summer after her collapse in Paris by solitary drinking. He is aware of an emptiness in himself where his feeling for her ought to be. Fitzgerald comments on the effects of emotional and psychological damage: 'There are open wounds, shrunk sometimes to the size of a pin-prick but wounds still' (p. 186).

While their life on the Riviera represents Dick's deterioration, the freedom offered by a life lived in the sun is given increasing symbolic significance for Nicole.

Nicole's garden

It is in the garden that Nicole seems to come into her own. Alone, she wanders through this part of the Villa Diana she has made her domain,

between kaleidoscopic peonies massed in pink clouds, black and brown tulips and fragile mauve-stemmed roses, transparent like sugar flowers in a confectioner's window – until, as if the scherzo of color could reach no further intensity, it broke off suddenly in mid-air, and moist steps went down to a level five feet below [Book I, p. 35].

When, later that night, the dinner-party at the Villa Diana breaks up, Nicole is last glimpsed by Rosemary 'blooming away and filling the night with graciousness' (p. 48). She is increasingly associated with the growth and sunshine of the Riviera. This is *her* world. Her only creative act in Switzerland is, significantly, the design of metal window bars elegantly disguised as flowers (Book II, p. 201). They imprison her, as well as the other patients.

After their return to the Riviera in 1929 (Book III), Nicole is again among growing things, and once more is referred to as 'blooming', but the word has a different resonance this time. Nicole is now moving towards full recovery: she is finding her true self as an attractive young woman at the height of her good looks and sexual power. After the meeting with Tommy Barban on Golding's yacht, she realizes how much Tommy desires her, and she makes her first bid for freedom by throwing the camphor rub to him when Dick has told her not to (p. 299). Just before this (p. 297) she goes alone into her garden, and Fitzgerald makes deliberate use of flower imagery:

Nicole went on through her garden routine ... Reaching the sea wall she fell into a communicative mood and no one to communicate with; so she stopped and deliberated. She was somewhat shocked at the idea of being interested in another man – but other women have lovers – why not me? In the fine spring morning the inhibitions of the male world disappeared and she reasoned as gaily as a flower, while the wind blew her hair until her head moved with it ... Why shouldn't I?

She asserts herself even further the next day by leaving Dick in disgust on the beach and driving the car home herself. Her 'blooming' is given a new significance: 'Her ego began blooming like a great rich rose as she scrambled back along the labyrinths in which she had wandered for years' (p. 310). It is noticeable that in the first of these two quotations personal morality is an attribute of the 'male world'. Fitzgerald makes some gender discriminations in this novel which have already been mentioned. Here he employs traditional associations of the garden with growth, femininity and fertility to denote the development of Nicole's sense of herself as a woman who wants to be loved passionately as Dick can no longer love her. Through all these years she has existed in the relation of child to Dick's father-figure, controlled by him and living the life he chose for her. Now with Tommy Barban she is ready to be her 'true self' (p. 314). As she prepares herself for her first night with Tommy she makes 'her person into the trimmest of gardens' (p. 312).

The Mediterranean sun, the garden and the beach are liberating forces for Nicole. Not only does she find sexual maturity and passion with Tommy Barban, she also retrieves her lost world and is able to slip easily into the world of the very rich on the Riviera: 'All summer she had been stimulated by watching people do exactly what they were tempted to do and pay no penalty for it' (p. 313). Nicole is reborn; she has 'cut the cord forever' (p. 324), meaning the umbilical cord, and again the metaphor is female in its implications. When Nicole meets Tommy Barban again on Golding's yacht the orchestra is playing 'I'm yours for the asking – but till then / You can't ask me to behave' (p. 289). There are no constraints upon her on the Riviera in 1929.

For Dick, the return to the Riviera completes his alienation. While Nicole enjoys liberation, he becomes increasingly imprisoned within his internal drama of defeat and self-accusation.

Changing points of view: an important structural feature

The use of the authorial voice is a narrative device for achieving an ironic detachment from the characters. But Fitzgerald employs the eyes and consciousness of three characters – Rosemary, then Dick, and finally Nicole – as the location of narrative interest. The order in which the three become the centre of consciousness is important.

Rosemary's consciousness

In the opening chapter of Book I Rosemary's inexperienced eye casts a glamour over the figures on the beach and over their life-style. She is young, just beginning to enjoy stardom and wealth. She finds a quality in these American men – Dick, Abe North and Tommy Barban – that she has not experienced in the film studios or among college boys, and she is charmed by it. She is sexually drawn to them and attracted by their maturity.

Dick is the one singled out, and Nicole, who is used to this, watches her fall in love with him 'with a little sigh at the fact that he was already possessed' (Book I, p. 28). Yet the authorial voice frequently interposes with a caution that Rosemary is not intellectually equipped to probe or speculate. Of her reactions to the Divers the reader is warned:

Her immature mind made no speculations upon the nature of their relation to each other, she was only concerned with their attitude toward herself – but she perceived the web of some pleasant inter-relation, which she expressed with the thought that they seemed to have a very good time [p. 27].

The phrase 'a very good time' exactly catches the childish language she would use. When Dick plays his 'pansy's trick' of emerging in what appear to be black lace swimming-trunks just to shock the bourgeois new arrivals (p. 30), Rosemary bubbles with delight. Again, the authorial voice warns the reader to beware of her facile acceptance of 'the expensive simplicity of the Divers', which conceals a desperate bid for happiness and a lack of innocence (p. 30). While Rosemary, with her enthusiasms and gushes of immature feeling, is engaged in finding a role that suits her, she is also effecting a 'final severance of the umbilical cord' (p. 50) from her mother through her first adult affair. Rosemary only notices the things that interest her, and, apart from Nicole's possessions, it is primarily Dick who engages her attention.

Dick's consciousness

It is both interesting and significant that the narrative enters Dick's consciousness at the point where he begins to lose control of the situation. The narrative thus penetrates, for the first time, Dick's façade of the smiling, charming manipulator of life, the 'conspirator for pleasure, mischief, profit, and delight' (Book III, p. 288) with whom Rosemary has been infatuated. On the beach in Book III when Rosemary resumes her old game of flattery and tells him that the rumours that he has changed are simply not true, Dick replies: 'It is true ... The change came a long way back – but at first it didn't show. The manner remains intact for some time after the morale cracks' (p. 307).

Dick's consciousness dominates the narrative from Chapter XX, Book I, onwards, until Nicole's takes over. The reader is hardly aware that the shift takes place in the shooting scene in the Paris station. Rosemary has just made a particularly silly and inadequate comment designed to bring the spotlight on to herself. After all, a man has just been shot dead, but Rosemary sighs:

'Sometimes I think I'm the most selfish person in the world.'
For the first time the mention of her mother annoyed rather than amused Dick.

He wanted to sweep away her mother, remove the whole affair from the nursery footing upon which Rosemary persistently established it. But he realized that this impulse was a loss of control – what would become of Rosemary's urge toward him if, for even a moment, he relaxed. He saw, not without panic, that the affair was sliding to rest; it could not stand still, it must go on or go back; for the first time it occurred to him that Rosemary had her hand on the lever more authoritatively than he [pp. 96–7].

The narrative enters Dick's consciousness at this point, though for the rest of Book I and much of Book II 'the manner remains intact'. The shooting has repercussions on all of them, but the focusing of the narrative on Dick's interior world gives prominence to its effect on him. His consciousness dominates the novel, and his perceptions and understanding shape the plot in the middle section. The reader judges other characters through the perspective of Dick's critical intelligence and moral values. The painful process of deterioration and self-knowledge that he undergoes could only be narrated through his consciousness as it is a very private one. Dick communicates nothing to the other characters.

Nicole's consciousness

When Nicole's consciousness predominates in the second Riviera section, in Book III, she provides an analysis of the situation which is based on her understanding of Dick and of her own position. Thus the innocence characterizing the opening book gives way to the deeper and more probing perceptions of the final one. Even though the story becomes superficially Nicole's story, it is actually Dick's which is the primary source of interest, since she is acutely aware of him and her new freedom is a reflection of his withdrawal and deterioration. She knows he is effecting a break with her, and through her thoughts the background of their life together is filled in:

The figures of Dick and herself, mutating [i.e. changing], undefined, appeared as spooks caught up into a fantastic dance. For months every word had seemed to have an overtone of some other meaning, soon to be resolved under circumstances that Dick would determine [pp. 300–301].

Just as Rosemary, in Book I, has a few scenes from which Dick is absent, so for the first time here Nicole is involved in a scene in which Dick is not present, when she begins her affair with Tommy Barban. Otherwise Dick holds the central place in the novel and the characters exist through their relationship with him. His personality and his presence are pivotal.

By placing Nicole's consciousness in the foreground of the narrative in the final chapter, Fitzgerald effects Dick's withdrawal but keeps him still the centre of interest. Nicole is beginning to enjoy the power her wealth and sexuality give her, and the use of her consciousness in this section of the novel emphasizes the gulf that now separates her from Dick. The last chapter on the beach (pp. 334–7) moves between them, rather as a film camera might, as a means of controlling the tensions of Dick's departure. First he is distanced from the reader by the formal reference to 'Doctor Diver' (p. 334). Then the narrative moves to Nicole and Baby Warren discussing him, the latter contemptuously dismissing even the memory of him:

'We should have let him confine himself to his bicycle excursions,' she remarked. 'When people are taken out of their depths they lose their heads, no matter how charming a bluff they put up.'
'Dick was a good husband to me for six years,' Nicole said [p. 335].

Then Dick is placed in the centre of interest again as he watches the sisters in the distance and talks over old times with Mary Minghetti, who begins to moralize and tell Dick where he went wrong. It is a measure of Fitzgerald's skill as a novelist that he is able to control the poignancy of Dick's loss of everything that has been dear to him by creating a sense of irony in this scene, highlighting Dick's moral superiority over Baby Warren, Mary and all the pleasure-seekers on the beach. When Mary tells Dick, 'All people want is to have a good time and if you make them unhappy you cut yourself off from nourishment' (p. 336), the reader perceives the irony of this, just as Dick does. The narrative shifts finally to Nicole, who wants to go and help him but is restrained by Tommy Barban with 'Let well enough alone' (p. 337).

The final chapter (pp. 337–8) employs Nicole's consciousness as a means of defining Dick's failure to achieve either professional status or personal peace. His continued restlessness, indicative of his alienation, is charted over a number of years by such phrases as: 'By accident she heard …'; 'she got the impression that …'; 'She looked up Geneva in an atlas'. The amount of information available to her diminishes until finally there is only supposition, presented by the author in a neutral tone and not necessarily attributed to Nicole: 'in any case he is almost certainly in that section of the country, in one town or another' (p. 338).

The pain of Dick's failure and disintegration is the central issue in the novel, yet Fitzgerald retains the note of irony which was present from the start of Book II. Dick allows himself to be seduced by his own attractiveness to women and by the attractions of wealth. The structure

100

of the novel brings into sharp and significant focus Dick's relationship with women and with the dazzling power of wealth.

In a letter written at the time of publication, Fitzgerald referred to *Tender is the Night* as a 'philosophical, now called psychological, novel', and commented:

... there were moments all through the book where I could have pointed up dramatic scenes, and I *deliberately* refrained from doing so because the material itself was so harrowing and highly charged that I did not want to subject the reader to a series of nervous shocks in a novel that was inevitably close to whoever read it in my generation.[3]

Whether readers are quite so vulnerable is open to question, but undoubtedly everyone today can understand Dick Diver's sources of strain and tension. The dilemma of the personality torn in two by conflicting impulses and deprived of the support of traditional shared beliefs and value systems is a contemporary one. The reader today can thus appreciate the technical experiments Fitzgerald carried out in order to express this complex psychological state.

Notes

1. *Tender is the Night*: A Novel of the 1920s

1. Andrew Turnbull (ed.), *The Letters of F. Scott Fitzgerald*, Penguin Books (1968), pp. 453–4.
2. André Le Vot, *F. Scott Fitzgerald: A Biography*, Penguin Books (1985), p. 77.
3. Ibid., p. 107.
4. Ibid., p. 210.
5. Matthew J. Bruccoli, *The Composition of Tender is the Night*, University of Pittsburgh Press (1963), p. xiii.
6. *Letters*, p. 301.
7. Malcolm Cowley's preface to the 1955 Penguin edition of *Tender is the Night*, p. 12.
8. Paul Fussell, *The Great War and Modern Memory*, Oxford University Press (1975), p. 12.
9. Ibid., p. 13.
10. Ibid., p. 14.
11. Ibid., p. 21.
12. *Letters*, pp. 256–7.

2. The Time-scheme of the Novel

1. For example:

Nicole's Age

Always one year younger than century.
Born July 1901
    courtship for two and one half years before that, since she was 13.
Catastrophe June 1917 Age almost 16
Clinic   Feb. 1918 Age 17
             To middle October bad period
             After Armistice good period
             He returns in April or May 1919
             She discharged June 1, 1919. Almost 18
             Married September 1919. Aged 18
Child born August 1920
Child born June 1922 . . .
In July 1929 when the story ends she is just 28

Quoted by Bruccoli, pp. 79–80.

102

3. Dick Diver

1. *The Crack-Up with Other Pieces and Stories*, Penguin Books (1965), pp. 11, 15.
2. Ibid., pp. 16–17.
3. Ibid., p. 18.
4. Ibid., p. 58.
5. Ibid., p. 59.
6. Ibid., p. 62.
7. Ibid., p. 63.
8. Ibid., p. 40.
9. Ibid., p. 39.
10. Ibid., p. 42.
11. Ibid., p. 46.
12. Ibid., p. 51.
13. Ibid., p. 50.
14. Ibid., p. 53.
15. Ibid., p. 55.
16. Ibid., p. 56.
17. Quoted by Malcolm Cowley in his preface to the 1955 edition of the novel.

4. Women Characters: 'You Are Attractive to Women, Dick'

1. In the context of Baby's character, 'frigid' would probably be the best interpretation of this term.
2. When the mind represses its guilty desires, the unconscious self may build up delusions which seem like reality. If these take over the personality, schizophrenia may result. Under treatment, the patient may 'transfer' the conflict on to the psychiatrist, and as Nicole's conflict centres on her father, she casts Dick in that role. The word is used later in Book III when Nicole turns to Tommy Barban, and again carries something of the same meaning.
3. Quoted by Bruccoli, p. 84.

5. The Structure of *Tender is the Night*

1. *Letters*, p. 529.
2. Abe North's rather enigmatic comment to Rosemary on the night of the duel, 'Plagued by the nightingale' (Book I, p. 52), is presumably an ironic reference to this. As there really is no reason why he should refer to it, more probably Fitzgerald wanted to underline the association with the previous moonlit scene.
3. *Letters*, p. 383.

Selected Reading

Works by Scott Fitzgerald

This Side of Paradise, Penguin Books, 1963.
The Beautiful and Damned, Penguin Books, 1966.
The Great Gatsby, Penguin Books, 1950.
The Last Tycoon, Penguin Books, 1965.
The Diamond as Big as the Ritz and Other Stories, Penguin Books, 1962.
The Crack-Up with Other Pieces and Stories, Penguin Books, 1965.
The Letters of F. Scott Fitzgerald, ed. Andrew Turnbull, Penguin Books, 1968.

Secondary reading

Bruccoli, Matthew J., *The Composition of Tender is the Night*, University of Pittsburgh Press, 1963. This extremely helpful work offers meticulous biographical research, some penetrating judgements and a useful bibliography.

Fussell, Paul, *The Great War and Modern Memory*, Oxford University Press, 1975. This study of the impact of the Great War on writers uses a range of valuable material illustrating shifts in opinion.

Le Vot, André *F. Scott Fitzgerald: A Biography*, Penguin Books, 1985. This critical biography gives a very detailed, balanced and sympathetic account of Fitzgerald's personal and professional life.

MORE ABOUT PENGUINS, PELICANS AND PUFFINS

For further information about books available from Penguins please write to Dept EP, Penguin Books Ltd, Harmondsworth, Middlesex UB7 0DA.

In the U.S.A.: For a complete list of books available from Penguins in the United States write to Dept DG, Penguin Books, 299 Murray Hill Parkway, East Rutherford, New Jersey 07073.

In Canada: For a complete list of books available from Penguins in Canada write to Penguin Books Canada Limited, 2801 John Street, Markham, Ontario L3R 1B4.

In Australia: For a complete list of books available from Penguins in Australia write to the Marketing Department, Penguin Books Australia Ltd, P.O. Box 257, Ringwood, Victoria 3134.

In New Zealand: For a complete list of books available from Penguins in New Zealand write to the Marketing Department, Penguin Books (N.Z.) Ltd, Private Bag, Takapuna, Auckland 9.

In India: For a complete list of books available from Penguins in India write to Penguin Overseas Ltd, 706 Eros Apartments, 56 Nehru Place, New Delhi 110019.

Other Penguins by F. Scott Fitzgerald

THE GREAT GATSBY

No one ever rightly knew who Gatsby was. Some said that he had been a German spy, others that he was related to one of Europe's Royal families. Despite this nearly everyone took advantage of his fabulous hospitality. And it really was fabulous. On his superb Long Island home he gave the most amazing parties, and not the least remarkable thing about them was the fact that few people could recognize their host. He seemed to be a person without background, without history, without a home. Yet the irony of this bright and brittle façade was that he had created it not to impress the world and his wife, but to impress just one person – a girl he had loved and had had to leave, a girl who had loved him but was now married to a rich good-for-nothing, a girl whom he had dreamed about for over four years. This dream had long ceased to have any substance or any connection with reality – and for that reason he could not wake from it. He had doped himself with his own illusion and only death could dispel that dream.

'It has interested and excited me more than any new novel I have seen, either English or American, for a number of years' – T. S. Eliot in a letter to the author in 1925.

Also published

The Beautiful and Damned
The Last Tycoon
Tender is the Night
Collected Short Stories in 5 volumes
This Side of Paradise
Bits of Paradise (with Zelda Fitzgerald)

Penguin Masterstudies

This comprehensive list, designed to help advanced level studies, includes:

Subjects

Applied Mathematics
Biology
Drama: Text into Performance
Geography
Pure Mathematics

Literature

Dr Faustus
Eugenie Grandet
The Great Gatsby
The Mill on the Floss
A Passage to India
Persuasion
Portrait of a Lady
Tender Is the Night
Vanity Fair
The Waste Land

Chaucer

The Knight's Tale
The Miller's Tale
The Nun's Priest's Tale
The Pardoner's Tale
The Prologue to The Canterbury Tales
A Chaucer Handbook

Shakespeare

Hamlet
King Lear
Measure for Measure
Othello
The Tempest
A Shakespeare Handbook

THE PENGUIN ENGLISH DICTIONARY

The Penguin English Dictionary has been created specially for today's needs. It features:

* More entries than any other popularly priced dictionary
* Exceptionally clear and precise definitions
* For the first time in an equivalent dictionary, the internationally recognised IPA pronunciation system
* Emphasis on contemporary usage
* Extended coverage of both the spoken and the written word
* Scientific tables
* Technical words
* Informal and colloquial expressions
* Vocabulary most widely used *wherever* English is spoken
* Most commonly used abbreviations

It is twenty years since the publication of the last English dictionary by Penguin and the compilation of this entirely new *Penguin English Dictionary* is the result of a special collaboration between Longman, one of the world's leading dictionary publishers, and Penguin Books. The material is based entirely on the database of the acclaimed *Longman Dictionary of the English Language.*

1008 pages   051.139 3   £2.50 ☐

ENGLISH AND AMERICAN
LITERATURE IN PENGUINS

☐ *Emma* **Jane Austen** £1.25

'I am going to take a heroine whom no one but myself will much like,' declared Jane Austen of Emma, her most spirited and controversial heroine in a comedy of self-deceit and self-discovery.

☐ *Tender is the Night* **F. Scott Fitzgerald** £2.95

Fitzgerald worked on seventeen different versions of this novel, and its obsessions – idealism, beauty, dissipation, alcohol and insanity – were those that consumed his own marriage and his life.

☐ *The Life of Johnson* **James Boswell** £2.95

Full of gusto, imagination, conversation and wit, Boswell's immortal portrait of Johnson is as near a novel as a true biography can be, and still regarded by many as the finest 'life' ever written. This shortened version is based on the 1799 edition.

☐ *A House and its Head* **Ivy Compton-Burnett** £4.95

In a novel 'as trim and tidy as a hand-grenade' (as Pamela Hansford Johnson put it), Ivy Compton-Burnett penetrates the facade of a conventional, upper-class Victorian family to uncover a chasm of violent emotions – jealousy, pain, frustration and sexual passion.

☐ *The Trumpet Major* **Thomas Hardy** £1.50

Although a vein of unhappy unrequited love runs through this novel, Hardy also draws on his warmest sense of humour to portray Wessex village life at the time of the Napoleonic wars.

☐ *The Complete Poems of Hugh MacDiarmid*

☐ Volume One £8.95
☐ Volume Two £8.95

The definitive edition of work by the greatest Scottish poet since Robert Burns, edited by his son Michael Grieve, and W. R. Aitken.

ENGLISH AND AMERICAN LITERATURE IN PENGUINS

☐ *Main Street* **Sinclair Lewis** £4.95

The novel that added an immortal chapter to the literature of America's Mid-West, *Main Street* contains the comic essence of Main Streets everywhere.

☐ *The Compleat Angler* **Izaak Walton** £2.50

A celebration of the countryside, and the superiority of those in 1653, as now, who love *quietnesse, vertue* and, above all, *Angling*. 'No fish, however coarse, could wish for a doughtier champion than Izaak Walton' – Lord Home

☐ *The Portrait of a Lady* **Henry James** £2.50

'One of the two most brilliant novels in the language', according to F. R. Leavis, James's masterpiece tells the story of a young American heiress, prey to fortune-hunters but not without a will of her own.

☐ *Hangover Square* **Patrick Hamilton** £3.95

Part love story, part thriller, and set in the publands of London's Earls Court, this novel caught the conversational tone of a whole generation in the uneasy months before the Second World War.

☐ *The Rainbow* **D. H. Lawrence** £2.50

Written between *Sons and Lovers* and *Women in Love*, *The Rainbow* covers three generations of Brangwens, a yeoman family living on the borders of Nottinghamshire.

☐ *Vindication of the Rights of Woman*
Mary Wollstonecraft £2.95

Although Walpole once called her 'a hyena in petticoats', Mary Wollstonecraft's vision was such that modern feminists continue to go back and debate the arguments so powerfully set down here.

ENGLISH AND AMERICAN
LITERATURE IN PENGUINS

☐ *Nostromo* **Joseph Conrad** £1.95

In his most ambitious and successful novel Conrad created an entire imaginary republic in South America. As he said, 'you shall find there according to your deserts: encouragement, consolation, fear, charm – all you demand – and, perhaps, also that glimpse of truth for which you forgot to ask.'

☐ *A Passage to India* **E. M. Forster** £2.50

Centred on the unsolved mystery at the Marabar Caves, Forster's masterpiece conveys, as no other novel has done, the troubled spirit of India during the Raj.

These books should be available at all good bookshops or news-agents, but if you live in the UK or the Republic of Ireland and have difficulty in getting to a bookshop, they can be ordered by post. Please indicate the titles required and fill in the form below.

NAME_____ BLOCK CAPITALS

ADDRESS_____

_____

_____

Enclose a cheque or postal order payable to The Penguin Bookshop to cover the total price of books ordered, plus 50p for postage. Readers in the Republic of Ireland should send £IR equivalent to the sterling prices, plus 67p for postage. Send to: The Penguin Bookshop, 54/56 Bridlesmith Gate, Nottingham, NG1 2GP.

You can also order by phoning (0602) 599295, and quoting your Barclaycard or Access number.

Every effort is made to ensure the accuracy of the price and availability of books at the time of going to press, but it is sometimes necessary to increase prices and in these circumstances retail prices may be shown on the covers of books which may differ from the prices shown in this list or elsewhere. This list is not an offer to supply any book.

This order service is only available to residents in the UK and the Republic of Ireland.